interchange

FOURTH EDITION

Jack C. Richards

With Jonathan Hull and Susan Proctor

Series Editor: David Bohlke

CAMBRIDGE
UNIVERSITY PRESS

STUDENT'S BOOK **2**

CAMBRIDGE UNIVERSITY PRESS
Cambridge, New York, Melbourne, Madrid, Cape Town,
Singapore, São Paulo, Delhi, Mexico City

Cambridge University Press
32 Avenue of the Americas, New York, NY 10013-2473, USA

www.cambridge.org
Information on this title: www.cambridge.org/9781107648692

© Cambridge University Press 2013

First published 1991
Second edition 2007
Third edition 2005
4th printing 2013

Printed in Hong Kong, China, by Golden Cup Printing Company Limited

A catalog record for this publication is available from the British Library.

ISBN 978-1-107-64869-2 Student's Book 2 with Self-study DVD-ROM
ISBN 978-1-107-64410-6 Student's Book 2A with Self-study DVD-ROM
ISBN 978-1-107-62676-8 Student's Book 2B with Self-study DVD-ROM
ISBN 978-1-107-64873-9 Workbook 2
ISBN 978-1-107-61698-1 Workbook 2A
ISBN 978-1-107-65075-6 Workbook 2B
ISBN 978-1-107-62527-3 Teacher's Edition 2 with Assessment Audio CD/CD-ROM
ISBN 978-1-107-62941-7 Class Audio 2 CDs
ISBN 978-1-107-62500-6 Full Contact 2 with Self-study DVD-ROM
ISBN 978-1-107-63719-1 Full Contact 2A with Self-study DVD-ROM
ISBN 978-1-107-65092-3 Full Contact 2B with Self-study DVD-ROM

For a full list of components, visit www. cambridge.org/interchange

Art direction, book design, layout services, and photo research: Integra
Audio production: CityVox, NYC
Video production: Nesson Media Boston, Inc.

Welcome to *Interchange Fourth Edition*, the world's most successful English series!

Interchange offers a complete set of tools for learning how to communicate in English.

Student's Book

with NEW Self-study DVD-ROM

- **Complete video program** with additional **video exercises**

- Additional **vocabulary**, **grammar, speaking, listening**, and **reading** practice
- Printable **score reports** to submit to teachers

Available online

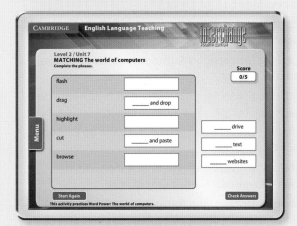

Interchange Arcade

- **Free** self-study website
- **Fun**, interactive, self-scoring activities
- Practice **vocabulary**, **grammar**, **listening**, and **reading**
- **MP3s** of the class audio program

Online Workbook

- A variety of **interactive activities** that correspond to each Student's Book lesson
- **Instant feedback** for hundreds of activities
- **Easy to use** with clear, easy-to-follow instructions
- Extra **listening practice**
- Simple tools for teachers to **monitor progress** such as scores, attendance, and time spent online

Authors' acknowledgments

A great number of people contributed to the development of *Interchange Fourth Edition*. Particular thanks are owed to the reviewers using *Interchange, Third Edition* in the following schools and institutes – their insights and suggestions have helped define the content and format of the fourth edition:

Ian Geoffrey Hanley, **The Address Education Center**, Izmir, Turkey

James McBride, **AUA Language Center**, Bangkok, Thailand

Jane Merivale, **Centennial College**, Toronto, Ontario, Canada

Elva Elena Peña Andrade, **Centro de Auto Aprendizaje de Idiomas**, Nuevo León, Mexico

José Paredes, **Centro de Educación Continua de la Escuela Politécnica Nacional** (CEC-EPN), Quito, Ecuador

Chia-jung Tsai, **Changhua University of Education**, Changhua City, Taiwan

Kevin Liang, **Chinese Culture University**, Taipei, Taiwan

Roger Alberto Neira Perez, **Colegio Santo Tomás de Aquino**, Bogotá, Colombia

Teachers at **Escuela Miguel F. Martínez**, Monterrey, Mexico

Maria Virgínia Goulart Borges de Lebron, **Great Idiomas**, São Paulo, Brazil

Gina Kim, **Hoseo University**, Chungnam, South Korea

Heeyong Kim, Seoul, South Korea

Elisa Borges, **IBEU-Rio**, Rio de Janeiro, Brazil

Jason M. Ham, **Inha University**, Incheon, South Korea

Rita de Cássia S. Silva Miranda, **Instituto Batista de Idiomas**, Belo Horizonte, Brazil

Teachers at **Instituto Politécnico Nacional**, Mexico City, Mexico

Victoria M. Roberts and Regina Marie Williams, **Interactive College of Technology**, Chamblee, Georgia, USA

Teachers at **Internacional de Idiomas**, Mexico City, Mexico

Marcelo Serafim Godinho, **Life Idiomas**, São Paulo, Brazil

J. Kevin Varden, **Meiji Gakuin University**, Yokohama, Japan

Rosa Maria Valencia Rodrìguez, Mexico City, Mexico

Chung-Ju Fan, **National Kinmen Institute of Technology**, Kinmen, Taiwan

Shawn Beasom, **Nihon Daigaku**, Tokyo, Japan

Gregory Hadley, **Niigata University of International and Information Studies**, Niigata, Japan

Chris Ruddenklau, **Osaka University of Economics and Law**, Osaka, Japan

Byron Roberts, **Our Lady of Providence Girls' High School**, Xindian City, Taiwan

Simon Banha, **Phil Young's English School**, Curitiba, Brazil

Flávia Gonçalves Carneiro Braathen, **Real English Center**, Viçosa, Brazil

Márcia Cristina Barboza de Miranda, **SENAC**, Recife, Brazil

Raymond Stone, **Seneca College of Applied Arts and Technology**, Toronto, Ontario, Canada

Gen Murai, **Takushoku University**, Tokyo, Japan

Teachers at **Tecnológico de Estudios Superiores de Ecatepec**, Mexico City, Mexico

Teachers at **Universidad Autónoma Metropolitana–Azcapotzalco**, Mexico City, Mexico

Teachers at **Universidad Autónoma de Nuevo León**, Monterrey, Mexico

Mary Grace Killian Reyes, **Universidad Autónoma de Tamaulipas**, Tampico Tamaulipas, Mexico

Teachers at **Universidad Estatal del Valle de Ecatepec**, Mexico City, Mexico

Teachers at **Universidad Nacional Autónoma de Mexico – Zaragoza**, Mexico City, Mexico

Teachers at **Universidad Nacional Autónoma de Mexico – Iztacala**, Mexico City, Mexico

Luz Edith Herrera Diaz, Veracruz, Mexico

Seri Park, **YBM PLS**, Seoul, South Korea

Self-assessment charts revised by Alex Tilbury

Grammar plus written by Karen Davy

CLASSROOM LANGUAGE *Student questions*

Plan of Book 2

Pronunciation/Listening	Writing/Reading	Interchange Activity
Reduced form of *used to* Listening to people talk about their past	Writing a paragraph about your childhood "Drew Barrymore: Actor, Producer, Director": Reading about the life and work of this Hollywood star	"Class profile": Finding out about a classmate's childhood PAGE 114
Syllable stress Listening to a description of a transportation system	Writing an online post on a community message board about a local issue "New Ways of Getting Around": Reading about new transportation inventions	"Tourism campaign": Suggesting ways to attract tourists to a city PAGE 115
Unpronounced vowels Listening to people talk about capsule hotels	Writing an e-mail comparing two living spaces "Break those bad habits": Reading about ways to end bad habits	"Wishful thinking": Finding out about a classmate's wishes PAGE 116
Consonant clusters Listening to descriptions of foods	Writing a recipe "Food and Mood": Reading about how food affects the way we feel	"Is that so?": Surveying classmates about their experiences PAGE 117
Linked sounds with /w/ and /y/ Listening to travel advice	Writing a letter with travel suggestions "Volunteer Travel – A vacation with a difference": Reading about how volunteer vacations work	"Fun vacations": Deciding on a trip PAGES 118, 120
Stress in two-part verbs Listening to the results of a survey about family life	Writing a set of guidelines "How to Ask for a Favor": Reading about ways to ensure a positive response to requests for a favor	"That's no excuse!" Apologizing and making amends PAGE 119
Syllable stress Listening to a radio program; listening to people give suggestions for using technology	Writing an email asking for specific favors "Modern-Day Treasure Hunters": Reading about the new hobby of geocaching	"Talk radio": Giving advice to classmates PAGE 121
Stress and rhythm Listening to a description of Carnaval in Brazil	Writing an entry on a travel website about a cultural custom "Customs Around the World": Reading about interesting customs and cultural events	"Special occasions": Finding out how classmates celebrate special events PAGE 122

Pronunciation/Listening	Writing/Reading	Interchange Activity
Intonation in statements with time phrases Listening to people talk about changes	Writing a paragraph describing a person's past, present, and possible future "Are you in love?": Reading about the signs of being in love	"Consider the consequences": Agreeing and disagreeing with classmates
Unreleased and released /t/ and /d/ Listening to people talk about their job preferences	Writing a cover letter for a job application "Find the Job That's Right for You!": Reading about how personality type affects career choices	"Dream job": Interviewing for a job
The letter o Listening to descriptions of monuments; listening for information about a country	Writing a guidebook introduction "A Guide to Unusual Museums": Reading about interesting museums	"Who is this by?": Sharing information about famous works
Contrastive stress in responses Listening to stories about unexpected experiences	Writing a description of a recent experience "From the Streets to the Screen": Reading about the rise of an unusual group of musicians	"Life is like a game!": Playing a board game to share past experiences
Emphatic stress Listening for opinions; listening to a movie review	Writing a movie review "Special Effects": Reading about the history of special effects	"Famous faces": Asking classmates' opinions about movies, TV shows, and celebrities
Pitch Listening to people talk about the meaning of signs	Writing a list of rules "Pearls of Wisdom": Reading about proverbs and their meaning	"What's going on?": Interpreting body language
Reduction of have Listening to people talk about predicaments; listening to a call-in radio show	Writing a letter to an advice columnist "The Advice Circle": Reading an online advice forum	"Do the right thing!": Deciding what to do in a difficult situation
Reduction of had and would Listening for excuses	Writing a report about people's responses to a survey; "The Truth About Lying": Reading about "white lies"	"Excuses, excuses": Discussing calendar conflicts and making up excuses

1 A time to remember

Friend Finder

Search

Ted Johnson

Sex: Male
Current city: Los Angeles, California, U.S.A.
Hometown: Dallas, Texas, U.S.A

Contact information
Email: ted.johnson@cup.org

Education and Work
College: **Farrington Technical Institute, Dallas**
Employer: **Deluxe Tours**

Likes and interests
I love to be outdoors. I enjoy skiing and swimming. And I'm a good cook.

Ana Fernandez

Sex: Female
Current city: Los Angeles, California, U.S.A.
Hometown: Buenos Aires, Argentina

Contact information
Email: a_fernandez@email.com

Education and Work
High school: **Santa Maria High School, Los Angeles**
Employer: **Sports Unlimited**

Likes and interests
I like to go to the movies and take long walks. And I'm learning to in-line skate!

Do you think Ted and Ana could be friends?
Is social networking popular in your country? Do you use any sites? Which ones?
Create your own online profile and compare it with a partner. How are you the same? different?

2 CONVERSATION *Where did you learn to skate?*

A ▶ Listen and practice.

Ted: Oh, I'm really sorry. Are you OK?
Ana: I'm fine. But I'm not very good at this.
Ted: Neither am I. . . . Hey, I like your shirt. Are you from Argentina?
Ana: Yes, I am, originally. I was born there.
Ted: Did you grow up there?
Ana: Yes, I did, but my family moved here ten years ago, when I was in middle school.
Ted: And where did you learn to skate?
Ana: Here in the park. This is only my third time.
Ted: Well, it's my *first* time. Can you give me some lessons?
Ana: Sure. Just follow me.
Ted: By the way, my name is Ted.
Ana: And I'm Ana. Nice to meet you.

B ▶ Listen to the rest of the conversation. What are two more things you learn about Ted?

3 GRAMMAR FOCUS

Past tense

Where **were** you born?	When **did** you **move** to Los Angeles?
I **was** born in Argentina.	I **moved** here ten years ago. I **didn't speak** English.
Were you born in Buenos Aires?	**Did** you **take** English classes in Argentina?
Yes, I **was**.	Yes, I **did**. I **took** classes for a year.
No, I **wasn't**. I **was** born in Córdoba.	No, I **didn't**. My aunt **taught** me at home.

A Complete these conversations. Then practice with a partner.

1. A: Could you tell me a little about yourself?
   Where .... you born?
   B: I .... born in South Korea.
   A: .... you grow up there?
   B: No, I .... I .... up in Canada.

2. A: When .... you begin to study English?
   B: I .... in middle school.
   A: What .... you think of English class
   at first?
   B: I .... it was a little difficult, but fun.

3. A: .... you have a favorite teacher when
   you .... a child?
   B: Yes, I .... I .... an excellent
   teacher named Miss Perez.
   A: What .... she teach?
   B: She .... science.

B **PAIR WORK** Take turns asking the questions in
part A. Give your own information when answering.

4 LISTENING *Life as an immigrant*

A ▶ Listen to interviews with two immigrants to the
United States. Where are they from?

B ▶ Listen again and complete the chart.

	Huy	Ahmed
1. When did he move to the United States?	....	....
2. What is difficult about being an immigrant?	....	....
3. What does he miss the most?	....	....

A time to remember ▪ **3**

5 SPEAKING Tell me about yourself.

A PAIR WORK Check (✓) six questions below. Then interview a classmate you don't know very well. Ask follow-up questions.

☐ Where did you go to middle school?
☐ Were you a good student in middle school?
☐ What were your best subjects?
☐ What subjects didn't you like?
☐ When did you first study English?

☐ What other languages can you speak?
☐ Do you have a big family?
☐ Did you enjoy your childhood?
☐ Did you have a pet?
☐ Who was your hero when you were a child?

A: What were your best subjects in middle school?
B: My best subjects were science and math.
A: Really? Me, too! Did you get good grades in English?

B GROUP WORK Tell the group what you learned about your partner. Then answer any questions.

"In middle school, Ji-won got good grades in science and math, but he didn't do very well in . . . "

useful expressions
Oh, that's interesting. Really? Me, too! Wow! Tell me more.

6 WORD POWER

A Complete the word map. Add two more words of your own to each category. Then compare with a partner.

✓ beach
cat
collect comic books
crayons
fish
play soccer
play video games
playground
rabbit
scrapbook
summer camp
toys

Pets
....
....
....
....
....

Hobbies
....
....
....
....
....

Childhood memories

Places
beach ....
....
....
....

Possessions
....
....
....
....

B PAIR WORK Choose three words from the word map and use them to describe some of your childhood memories.

A: I had a scrapbook when I was little.
B: What did you keep in it?
A: I kept lots of things in it. It had some school awards, photos, and notes from my friends.

7 PERSPECTIVES *How have you changed?*

A ▶ Listen to these statements about changes. Check (✓) those that are true about you.

☐ **1.** "When I was a kid, I used to be very messy, but now I'm very neat."

☐ **2.** "I didn't use to collect anything, but now I do."

☐ **3.** "I never used to play sports, but now I like to keep fit."

☐ **4.** "I never used to worry about money, but I do now."

☐ **5.** "I used to have a lot of hobbies, but now I don't have any free time."

☐ **6.** "I didn't use to follow politics, but now I check headlines online every day."

☐ **7.** "When I was younger, I used to care a lot about my appearance. Now, I'm too busy to care how I look."

B **PAIR WORK** Look at the statements again. Which changes are positive? Which are negative?

"I think the first one is a positive change. It's good to be neat."

8 GRAMMAR FOCUS

> ### Used to ▶
>
> **Used to** *refers to something that you regularly did in the past but don't do anymore.*
>
> **Did** you **use to** collect things?
>   Yes, I **used to** collect comic books.
>   No, I **didn't use to** collect anything,
>   but now I collect art.
>
> What sports **did** you **use to** play?
>   I **used to play** baseball and volleyball.
>   I **never used to** play sports, but now I
>   play tennis.

A Complete these questions and answers. Then compare with a partner.

1. A: ..Did.. you ......use to........ collect comic books when you were little?
   B: No, I .... collect comic books.

2. A: .... you and your friends .... play at the playground as kids?
   B: Yes, we .... spend hours there on the weekends.

3. A: What video games .... you .... play?
   B: I .... play video games. But now I play them all the time!

4. A: What music .... you .... listen to?
   B: I .... listen to pop music a lot, but now I prefer rock.

B How have you changed? Write six sentences about yourself using *used to* or *didn't use to*.

your hairstyle   your taste in music
your hobbies   the way you dress

> I used to wear my hair much longer.
> I didn't use to wear it short.

9 PRONUNCIATION Used to

A ▶ Listen and practice. Notice that the pronunciation of **used to** and **use to** is the same.

When I was a child, I **used to** play the trumpet.
I **used to** have a nickname.
I didn't **use to** like scary movies.
I didn't **use to** study very hard at school.

B **PAIR WORK** Practice the sentences you wrote in Exercise 8, part B. Pay attention to the pronunciation of **used to** and **use to**.

10 SPEAKING Memories

A **PAIR WORK** Add three questions to this list. Then take turns asking and answering the questions.

1. What's your favorite childhood memory?
2. What sports or games did you use to play when you were younger?
3. Did you use to have a nickname?
4. Where did you use to spend your vacations?
5. Is your taste in music different now?
6. ....
7. ....
8. ....

B **CLASS ACTIVITY** Tell the class two interesting things about your partner.

11 WRITING About myself

A Write a paragraph about things you used to do as a child. Use some of your ideas from Exercise 10. Just for fun, include one false statement.

> When I was four years old, my family moved to Australia. We had an old two-story house and a big yard. My older brother and I used to play lots of games together. In the summer, my favorite outdoor game was . . .

B **GROUP WORK** Share your paragraphs and answer any questions. Can you find the false statements?

12 INTERCHANGE 1 Class profile

Find out more about your classmates. Go to Interchange 1 on page 114.

DREW BARRYMORE — Actor, Producer, Director

Scan the article. Where was Drew Barrymore born? When did she start working? When did she win the Golden Globe Award?

Drew Barrymore was born in Los Angeles, California, in 1975. She comes from a long line of actors. In fact, her grandfather, John Barrymore, was one of the most famous actors in the United States in the 1920s.

Drew Barrymore began her career very early. Before her first birthday, she appeared in a TV commercial for dog food. At the age of two, she acted in her first TV movie. At age five, she appeared in her first feature film, the sci-fi thriller *Altered States*.

Barrymore's big break came two years later, at age seven. Director Steven Spielberg decided to cast her in his film *E.T.: The Extra-Terrestrial*. Hollywood took notice, and Drew became a star.

As a young adult, Barrymore acted in several dramas and romantic comedies; however, she wanted to make her own films. In 1995, she started her own production company, Flower Films. Four years later, she produced her first film, *Never Been Kissed*. Over the years, her company has made a lot of famous movies and TV programs, including *Fever Pitch* in 2005 and the new *Charlie's Angels* TV series in 2011.

In 2007, Barrymore's career took a new turn. She began working for the United Nations World Food Programme. Later, she donated $1 million to the program. Then, after a terrible earthquake in Haiti in 2010, she urged people to give money to the program in a YouTube video.

Meanwhile, Barrymore's work on movies continued. In 2009, she became a director with the film *Whip It*. In the same year, she won the Golden Globe Award as an actress for her role in *Grey Gardens*.

Drew Barrymore wears many different hats and works very long hours. What does she do in her free time? She spends time with the people she cares about. She says, "I don't know what I'd do without my friends."

A Read the article. Find the words in *italics* below in the article. Then circle the meaning of each word or phrase.

1. When you get a *big break*, you experience a sudden **advance / accident**.
2. To *cast* an actor means to **hire / fire** the actor.
3. A *production company* **trains young actors / makes films.**
4. If you *urged* someone to do something, you **encouraged / discouraged** him or her.
5. When an actor plays a *role* in a film, he or she **wins an award / acts as another person.**
6. When someone *wears many different hats*, he or she **does a lot of different jobs / wins a lot of different awards.**

B Number these sentences about Drew Barrymore from 1 (first event) to 10 (last event).

.... a. She became a film director.
.... b. She became a film producer.
.... c. She gave away $1 million.
.... d. She was in a TV commercial.
...1... e. She was born in California.
.... f. She started working for the United Nations.
.... g. She got her first role in a feature film.
.... h. She produced the movie *Fever Pitch*.
.... i. She became very famous as a child actor.
.... j. She started her own production company.

C **PAIR WORK** Who is your favorite actor or actress? What do you know about his or her life and career?

2 Caught in the rush

1 WORD POWER Compound nouns

A Match the words in columns A and B to make compound nouns. (More than one combination may be possible.)

subway + station = subway station

A	B
bicycle	garage
bus	jam
news	lane
parking	light
street	space
subway	stand
taxi	station
traffic	stop
train	system

a taxi stand

a bicycle lane

B PAIR WORK Which of these things can you find where you live?

A: There is a bus system here.
B: Yes. There are also a lot of traffic jams.

2 PERSPECTIVES Transportation services

A ▶ Listen to these comments about transportation services. Match them to the correct pictures.

_____ 1. "The buses are old and slow, and they cause too much pollution. In cities with less pollution, people are healthier."

_____ 2. "There are too many cars. All the cars, taxis, and buses are a danger to bicyclists. There is too much traffic!"

_____ 3. "There should be fewer cars, but I think that the biggest problem is parking. There just isn't enough parking."

B PAIR WORK Does your city or town have problems with traffic, pollution, and parking? What do you think is the biggest problem?

GRAMMAR FOCUS

> ### Expressions of quantity ⊙
>
> | With count nouns | With noncount nouns |
> |---|---|
> | There are **too many** cars. | There is **too much** traffic. |
> | There should be **fewer** cars. | There should be **less** pollution. |
> | We need **more** subway lines. | We need **more** public transportation. |
> | There are**n't enough** buses. | There is**n't enough** parking. |

A Complete these statements about transportation problems. Then compare with a partner. (More than one answer may be possible.)

1. There are .... police officers.
2. There should be .... cars in the city.
3. There is .... public transportation.
4. The government needs to build .... highways.
5. There should be .... noise.
6. The city needs .... public parking garages.
7. There is .... air pollution in the city.
8. There are .... cars parked on the streets.

B PAIR WORK Write sentences about the city or town you are living in. Then compare with another pair.

1. The city should provide more . . .
2. We have too many . . .
3. There's too much . . .
4. There isn't enough . . .
5. There should be fewer . . .
6. We don't have enough . . .
7. There should be less . . .
8. We need more . . .

4 **LISTENING** *Singapore solves it.*

A ⊙ Listen to a resident of Singapore talk about how his city has tried to solve its traffic problems. Check (✓) True or False for each statement.

True	False		
☐	✓	**1.** Motorists can't drive into the business district.	*They need a pass to drive there.*
☐	☐	**2.** People need a special certificate to buy a car.	....
☐	☐	**3.** There are enough certificates for everyone.	....
☐	☐	**4.** Cars are more expensive than in North America.	....
☐	☐	**5.** Public transportation isn't very good.	....

B ⊙ Listen again. For the false statements, write the correct information.

C CLASS ACTIVITY Could the solutions adopted in Singapore work in your city or town? Why or why not?

5 DISCUSSION *You be the judge!*

A GROUP WORK Which of these transportation services are available in your city or town? Discuss what is good and bad about each one.

.... taxi service
.... the bus system
.... the subway system
.... the train system
.... facilities for pedestrians
.... parking

B GROUP WORK How would you rate the transportation services where you live? Give each item a rating from 1 to 5.

1 = terrible   2 = needs improvement   3 = average   4 = good   5 = excellent

A: I'd give the taxi service a 4. There are enough taxis, but there are too many bad drivers.
B: I think a rating of 4 is too high. There should be more taxi stands and . . .

6 WRITING *An online post*

A Read this post from a community message board about traffic in the city.

B Use your statements from Exercise 3, part B, and any new ideas to write a message about a local issue.

C GROUP WORK Take turns reading your messages. Do you have any of the same concerns?

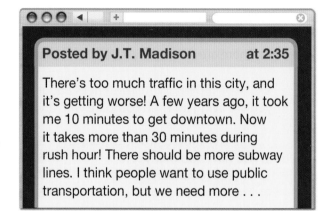

Posted by J.T. Madison   at 2:35

There's too much traffic in this city, and it's getting worse! A few years ago, it took me 10 minutes to get downtown. Now it takes more than 30 minutes during rush hour! There should be more subway lines. I think people want to use public transportation, but we need more . . .

7 SNAPSHOT

Common Questions
Asked by Visitors to a City

☐ How much do taxis cost?
☐ Where should I go shopping?
☐ Where can I get a map?
☐ What's the best way to see the city?
☐ Where can I buy a prepaid phone?

☐ Where's a good place to meet friends?
☐ What festivals or events are taking place?
☐ What are some family-friendly activities?
☐ Which hotel is closest to the airport?
☐ What museums should I see?

Sources: www.choosechicago.com; www.timessquarenyc.org

Check (✓) the questions you can answer about your city.
What other questions could a visitor ask about your city?
Talk to your classmates. Find answers to the questions you didn't check.

8 CONVERSATION *Could you tell me . . . ?*

A Listen and practice.

Eric: Excuse me. Could you tell me where the nearest ATM is?

Clerk: There's one upstairs, across from the duty-free shop.

Eric: Great. And do you know where I can catch a bus to the city?

Clerk: Sure. Just follow the signs for "Transportation."

Eric: OK. And can you tell me how often they run?

Clerk: They run every 20 minutes or so.

Eric: And just one more thing. Do you know where the restrooms are?

Clerk: Right behind you. Do you see where that sign is?

Eric: Oh. Thanks a lot.

B Listen to the rest of the conversation. Check (✓) the information that Eric asks for.

☐ the cost of a bus to the city ☐ the cost of a guidebook
☐ the location of a taxi stand ☐ the location of a bookstore

9 GRAMMAR FOCUS

Indirect questions from Wh-questions

Wh-questions with be	**Indirect questions**
Where is the nearest ATM?	Could you tell me **where the nearest ATM is**?
Where are the restrooms?	Do you know **where the restrooms are**?

Wh-questions with do	**Indirect questions**
How often do the buses run?	Can you tell me **how often the buses run**?
What time does the bookstore open?	Do you know **what time the bookstore opens**?

Wh-questions with can	**Indirect questions**
Where can I catch the bus?	Do you know **where I can catch the bus**?

A Write indirect questions using these Wh-questions. Then compare with a partner.

1. How much does the bus cost?
2. Where's the nearest Internet café?
3. What time do the banks open?
4. How late do the buses run?
5. Where can I get a quick meal?
6. How late do the nightclubs stay open?
7. How early do the trains run?
8. Where's an inexpensive hotel in this area?

B **PAIR WORK** Take turns asking the questions you wrote in part A. Give your own information when answering.

"Can you tell me how much the bus costs?"

10 PRONUNCIATION Syllable stress

A ▶ Listen and practice. Notice which syllable has the main stress in these two-syllable words.

● ○	○ ●
subway	garage
traffic	police

B ▶ Listen to the stress in these words. Write them in the correct columns. Then compare with a partner.

		● ○	○ ●
buses	improve	....	....
bookstore	provide	....	....
event	public	....	....
hotel	taxis	....	....

11 SPEAKING What do you know?

A Complete the chart with indirect questions.

	Name: ....
1. Where's the nearest bus stop? "_Do you know where_ .... ?"	....
2. What's the best way to see the city? " .... ?"	....
3. Where can I rent a bicycle? " .... ?"	....
4. How much does a city tour cost? " .... ?"	....
5. Where can I get a student discount on a meal? " .... ?"	....
6. What time do the museums open? " .... ?"	....
7. Where can I hear live music? " .... ?"	....

B PAIR WORK Use the indirect questions in the chart to interview a classmate about the city or town where you live. Take notes.

A: Do you know where the nearest bus stop is?
B: I'm not really sure, but I think there's one . . .

C CLASS ACTIVITY Share your answers with the class. Who knows the most about your city or town?

12 INTERCHANGE 2 Tourism campaign

Discuss ways to attract tourists to a city. Go to Interchange 2 on page 115.

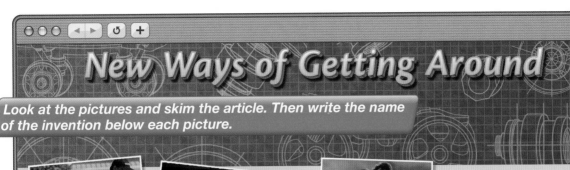

New Ways of Getting Around

Look at the pictures and skim the article. Then write the name of the invention below each picture.

Here are some of the best new inventions for getting around.

If you love to take risks when you travel, this is for you: the **Wheelman**. The design is simple: two wheels and a motor. You put your feet in the wheels. It's very similar to skateboarding or surfing. You use your weight to steer, and you control the speed with a ball you hold in your hand.

Why use two wheels when you can use three? The **Trikke Scooter** looks a little silly, but it's serious transportation. The three wheels make it very stable. And because it's made of aluminum, it's very light. It moves by turning back and forth – just like skiing on the street.

Do you want an eco-friendly family car? If so, check out the **Leaf**. It's all-electric and gives off zero CO_2 emissions. It has an 80 kW motor and can travel up to 140 kph! You can recharge the battery up to 80 percent of capacity in just 30 minutes and recharge it fully overnight.

To get around town in style and park easily, there's nothing better than the **Twizy Z.E.** It has four wheels, but it's only 2.3 meters long and 1.13 meters wide – the passenger sits behind the driver. It has a zero-emission 15 kW electric motor that can reach a maximum speed of 75 kph.

A Read the article. Where do you think it is from? Check (✓) the correct answer.

☐ an instruction manual   ☐ a catalog   ☐ a news magazine   ☐ an encyclopedia

B Answer these questions.

1. Which inventions have motors? ....
2. Where do you put your feet in the Wheelman? ....
3. How do you steer the Wheelman? ....
4. What is the Trikke Scooter made of? ....
5. How does the Trikke Scooter move? ....
6. How long does it take to fully recharge the Leaf? ....
7. How long is the Twizy Z.E.? ....
8. Where does the passenger sit in the Twizy Z.E.? ....

C GROUP WORK Which of the inventions is the most useful? the least useful? Why? Would you like to try any of them?

Units 1–2 Progress check

SELF-ASSESSMENT

How well can you do these things? Check (✓) the boxes.

I can	Very well	OK	A little
Understand descriptions of childhood (Ex. 1)	☐	☐	☐
Ask and answer questions about childhood and past times (Ex. 1, 2)	☐	☐	☐
Express opinions about cities and towns; agree and disagree (Ex. 3)	☐	☐	☐
Ask for and give information about a city or town (Ex. 4)	☐	☐	☐

1 LISTENING *Celebrity interview*

A ▶ Listen to an interview with Jeri, a fashion model. Answer the questions.

1. Where did she grow up? ....
2. What did she want to do when she grew up? ....
3. Did she have a hobby? ....
4. Did she have a favorite game? ....
5. What was her favorite place? ....

B PAIR WORK Use the questions in part A to interview a partner about his or her childhood. Ask follow-up questions to get more information.

2 DISCUSSION *How times have changed!*

A PAIR WORK Talk about how life in your country has changed in the last 50 years. Ask questions like these:

How big were families 50 years ago?
What kinds of homes did people live in?
How did people use to dress?
How were schools different?
What kinds of jobs did men have? women?
How much did people use to earn?

A: How big were families 50 years ago?
B: Families used to be much larger. My grandfather had ten brothers and sisters!

B GROUP WORK Compare your answers. Do you think life was better in the old days? Why or why not?

3 SURVEY *City planner*

A What do you think about these things in your city or town? Complete the survey.

	Not enough	OK	Too many/Too much
places to go dancing	☐	☐	☐
places to listen to music	☐	☐	☐
noise	☐	☐	☐
places to sit and have coffee	☐	☐	☐
places to go shopping	☐	☐	☐
parking	☐	☐	☐
public transportation	☐	☐	☐
places to meet new people	☐	☐	☐

B GROUP WORK Compare your opinions and suggest ways to make your city or town better. Then agree on three improvements.

A: How would you make our city better?
B: There aren't enough places to go dancing. We need more nightclubs.
C: I disagree. There should be fewer clubs. There's too much noise downtown!

4 ROLE PLAY *Getting information*

Student A: Imagine you are a visitor in your city or town. Write five indirect questions about these categories. Then ask your questions to the hotel front-desk clerk.

Transportation   Hotels
Restaurants   Sightseeing
Shopping   Entertainment

Student B: You are a hotel front-desk clerk. Answer the guest's questions. Start like this: *Can I help you?*

Change roles and try the role play again.

useful expressions
Let me think. Oh, yes, . . .
I'm not really sure, but I think . . .
Sorry, I don't know.

WHAT'S NEXT?

Look at your Self-assessment again. Do you need to review anything?

3 Time for a change!

WORD POWER *Houses and apartments*

A These words are used to describe houses and apartments. Which are positive (**P**)? Which are negative (**N**)?

bright

bright	..P..	dingy	....	private	....
comfortable	....	expensive	....	quiet	....
convenient	....	huge	....	safe	....
cramped	....	inconvenient	....	shabby	....
dangerous	....	modern	....	small	....
dark	....	noisy	....	spacious	....

B **PAIR WORK** Tell your partner two positive and two negative features of your house or apartment.

"I live in a safe neighborhood, and my apartment is very bright. However, it's very expensive and a little cramped."

2 **PERSPECTIVES** *Which would you prefer?*

A ▶ Listen to these opinions about houses and apartments. Which ones are about space?

1. Apartments are too small for pets.
2. Apartments aren't big enough for families.
3. Apartments don't have as many rooms as houses.
4. Apartments have just as many expenses as houses.
5. Apartments don't have enough parking spaces.

6. Houses cost too much money.
7. Houses aren't as safe as apartments.
8. Houses aren't as convenient as apartments.
9. Houses don't have enough closet space.
10. Houses don't have as much privacy as apartments.

B **PAIR WORK** Look at the opinions again. Which statements do you agree with?

A: I agree that apartments are too small for pets.
B: And they don't have enough parking spaces!

Evaluations and comparisons ▶

Evaluations with adjectives
Apartments are**n't** big **enough** for families.
Apartments are **too** small for pets.

Evaluations with nouns
Apartments do**n't** have **enough** parking spaces.
Houses cost **too much** money.

Comparisons with adjectives
Houses are**n't as** convenient **as** apartments.
Houses are **just as** convenient **as** apartments.

Comparisons with nouns
Apartments have **just as many** rooms **as** houses.
Apartments do**n't** have **as much** privacy **as** houses.

A Imagine you are looking for a house or an apartment to rent. Read the two ads. Then rewrite the opinions below using the words in parentheses. Compare with a partner.

Spacious, modern house
3 bedrooms, 1 bathroom; very private; in quiet suburb; 2-car garage; $1500 per month.

Smaller, older apartment
2 bedrooms, 1 bathroom; downtown, near subway; 1 parking space; $900 per month.

1. There are only a few windows. (not enough)
2. It's not bright enough. (too)
3. It has only one bathroom. (not enough)
4. It's not convenient enough. (too)

5. It's not spacious enough. (too)
6. It's too old. (not enough)
7. It isn't safe enough. (too)
8. There's only one parking space. (not enough)

> There aren't enough windows.

B Write comparisons of the house and the apartment using these words and *as . . . as*. Then compare with a partner.

noisy   big
bedrooms   expensive
bathrooms   modern
spacious   convenient
private   parking spaces

> The house isn't as noisy as the apartment.
> The apartment doesn't have as many bedrooms as the house.

C **GROUP WORK** Which would you prefer to rent, the house or the apartment? Why?

A: I'd rent the apartment because the house costs too much.
B: I'd choose the house. The apartment isn't big enough for my family.

4 PRONUNCIATION Unpronounced vowels

A ◉ Listen and practice. The vowel immediately after a stressed syllable is sometimes not pronounced.

● ○

av̶erage
diff̶erent
sep̶arate

● ○ ○

comf̶ortable
int̶eresting
veg̶etable

B Write four sentences using some of the words in part A. Then read them with a partner. Pay attention to unpronounced vowels.

> In my hometown, the average apartment has two bedrooms.

5 LISTENING Capsule hotels

A ◉ Listen to Brad describe a "capsule hotel." Check (✓) the words that best describe it.

☐ cramped ☐ convenient ☐ bright
☐ expensive ☐ busy ☐ dangerous

B ◉ Listen again. In addition to a bed, what does the hotel provide? Write four things.

....
....

C PAIR WORK Would you like to stay in a capsule hotel? Why or why not?

6 WRITING A descriptive email

A Imagine you've just moved to this apartment. Write an email to a friend comparing your old home to your new one.

○○○ ◀ ＋ ⊗

Dear Emma,

How are things with you? My big news is that I just moved to a new apartment! Do you remember my old apartment? It didn't have enough space. My new apartment has a huge living room and two bathrooms! Also, my old living room was too dark, but my new one is brighter. But there aren't enough windows in the bedrooms, so they're too dark. There are . . .

B PAIR WORK Read each other's emails. How are your descriptions similar? different?

7 SNAPSHOT

COMMON WISHES PEOPLE HAVE ABOUT THEIR LIVES

☐ IMPROVE MY PERSONALITY

☐ ENJOY LIFE MORE

☐ PLAY A MUSICAL INSTRUMENT

☐ FIND A BETTER JOB

☐ ADD MORE HOURS TO THE DAY

☐ GO BACK TO SCHOOL

☐ MOVE TO A NEW HOME

☐ MAKE SOME NEW FRIENDS

☐ SPEND MORE TIME WITH MY FAMILY

Source: Based on interviews with adults between the ages of 18 and 50

Check (✓) some of the things you would like to do. Then tell a partner why.
Which of these wishes would be easy to achieve? Which would be difficult or impossible?
What other things would you like to change about your life? Why?

8 CONVERSATION *Making changes*

A ⊙ Listen and practice.

Brian: So, are you still living with your parents, Terry?

Terry: I'm afraid so. I wish I had my own apartment.

Brian: Why? Don't you like living at home?

Terry: It's OK, but my parents are always asking me to be home before midnight. I wish they'd stop worrying about me.

Brian: Yeah, parents are like that!

Terry: And they expect me to help around the house. I hate housework. I wish life weren't so difficult.

Brian: So, why don't you move out?

Terry: Hey, I wish I could, but where else can I get free room and board?

B ⊙ Listen to the rest of the conversation. What changes would Brian like to make in his life?

Time for a change! ■ 19

9 GRAMMAR FOCUS

Wish ▶

Use wish + past tense to refer to present wishes.

I **live** with my parents.
    I wish I **didn't live** with my parents.
    I wish I **had** my own apartment.
I **can't move** out.
    I wish I **could move** out.

Life **is** difficult.
    I wish it **were*** easier.
    I wish it **weren't** so difficult.
My parents **won't stop** worrying about me.
    I wish they **would stop** worrying about me.

*For the verb be, were is used with all pronouns after wish.

A Read these facts about people's lives. Then rewrite the sentences using *wish*. (More than one answer is possible.)

1. Diane can't wear contact lenses.   *She wishes she could wear contact lenses.*
2. Beth's class is so boring.   *She wishes her class weren't so boring.*
3. My parents can't afford a new car.   ....
4. Dan can't fit into his old jeans.   ....
5. I can't remember my PIN number.   ....
6. Laura doesn't have any free time.   ....
7. Mitch is too short to play basketball.   ....

B PAIR WORK Think of five things you wish you could change. Then discuss them with your partner.

A: What do you wish you could change?
B: Well, I'm not in very good shape. I wish I were more fit.

10 SPEAKING *Wish list*

A What do you wish were different about these things? Write down your wishes.

my bedroom	my social life	my possessions
my school or job	my skills	my town

B GROUP WORK Compare your wishes. Does anyone have the same wish?

A: I wish my bedroom were a different color. It's not bright enough.
B: Me, too! I wish I could paint my bedroom bright orange.
C: I like the color of my bedroom, but my bed is too small. I wish . . .

11 INTERCHANGE 3 *Wishful thinking*

Find out more about your classmates' wishes. Go to Interchange 3 on page 116.

Break those bad habits

Skim the article. What three bad habits does the article mention?

Some people leave work until the last minute, a lot of us like to spread or listen to gossip, and others always arrive at events late. These aren't as serious as some problems, but they are bad habits that can cause trouble. Habits like these waste your time and, in some cases, might even affect your relationships. Do you wish you could break your bad habits? Read this advice to end these habits forever!

There's Always Tomorrow

1 *PROBLEM:* Do you leave projects until the very last minute and then stay up all night to finish them?

2 *SOLUTION:* People often put things off because they seem overwhelming. Try to divide the project into smaller steps. After you finish each task, reward yourself with a snack or a call to a friend.

Guess What I Just Heard

3 *PROBLEM:* Do you think it's not nice to talk about other people, but do it anyway? Do you feel bad after you've done it?

4 *SOLUTION:* First, never listen to gossip. If someone tries to tell you a secret, just say, "Sorry. I'm not really interested." Then think of some other news to offer – about yourself.

Never on Time

5 *PROBLEM:* Are you always late? Do your friends invite you to events a half hour early?

6 *SOLUTION:* Use the reminder function in your phone. For example, if a movie starts at 8:00 and it takes you 20 minutes to get to the theater, you have to leave by 7:40. Put the event in your phone calendar, and then set it to send you a reminder at 7:30.

A Read the article. Then check (✓) the best description of the article.

☐ 1. The article starts with a description and then gives advice.
☐ 2. The article starts with a description and then gives facts.
☐ 3. The article gives the writer's opinion.

B Where do these sentences belong? Write the number of the paragraph where each sentence could go.

.... a. You can also ask a friend to come to your home before the event.
.... b. Ask yourself: "How would I feel if someone told my secrets?"
.... c. Do you ever make up excuses to explain your unfinished work?
.... d. Are you ever so late that the people you're meeting decide to leave?
.... e. You can also ask a friend to call you to ask about your progress.
.... f. Are people afraid to tell you things about themselves?

C **PAIR WORK** Discuss other ways to break each of these bad habits.

4 I've never heard of that!

Favorite Ethnic Dishes

South Korea	Brazil	Morocco	Singapore
Bulgogi	**Feijoada**	**Lamb Tagine**	**Fish Head Curry**
Beef marinated with soy sauce and other spices	*A dish made of black beans, garlic, spices, and meat*	*A stew of vegetables, lamb, fruit, and spices cooked in a clay dish*	*A dish made from a fish head cooked in a rich curry sauce*

Sources: *Fodor's South America; Fodor's Southeast Asia;* www.globalgourmet.com

Which dishes are made with meat? with fish?
Have you ever tried any of these dishes? Which ones would you like to try?
What ethnic foods are popular in your country?

2 CONVERSATION *Have you ever . . . ?*

A ⊙ Listen and practice.

Steve: Hey, this sounds strange – snails with garlic. Have you ever eaten snails?
Kathy: Yes, I have. I had them here just last week.
Steve: Did you like them?
Kathy: Yes, I did. They were delicious! Why don't you try some?
Steve: No, I don't think so.
Server: Have you decided on an appetizer yet?
Kathy: Yes. I'll have a small order of the snails, please.
Server: And you, sir?
Steve: I think I'll have the fried brains.
Kathy: Fried brains? I've never heard of that! It sounds scary.

B ⊙ Listen to the rest of the conversation. How did Steve like the fried brains? What else did he order?

3 PRONUNCIATION *Consonant clusters*

A ▶ Listen and practice. Notice how the two consonants at the beginning of a word are pronounced together.

/k/	/t/	/m/	/n/	/p/	/r/	/l/
skim	start	smart	snack	spare	brown	blue
scan	step	smile	snow	speak	gray	play

B **PAIR WORK** Find one more word on page 22 for each consonant cluster in part A. Then practice saying the words.

4 GRAMMAR FOCUS

> ### Simple past vs. present perfect ▶
>
> *Use the simple past for experiences at a definite time in the past.*
> *Use the present perfect for experiences within a time period up to the present.*
>
> **Have** you ever **eaten** snails?
>   Yes, I **have**. I **tried** them last month.
> **Did** you **like** them?
>   Yes, I **did**. They **were** delicious.
>
> **Have** you ever **been** to a Vietnamese restaurant?
>   No, I **haven't**. But I **ate** at a Thai restaurant last night.
> **Did** you **go** alone?
>   No, I **went** with some friends.

A Complete these conversations. Then practice with a partner.

1. A: Have you ever ....*been*.... (be) to a picnic at the beach?
   B: Yes, I .... My family and I .... (have) a picnic on the beach last month. We .... (cook) hamburgers.

2. A: Have you ever .... (try) sushi?
   B: No, I .... , but I'd like to.

3. A: Did you .... (have) breakfast today?
   B: Yes, I .... I .... (eat) a huge breakfast.

4. A: Have you ever .... (eat) Mexican food?
   B: Yes, I .... In fact, I .... (eat) some just last week.

5. A: Did you .... (drink) coffee this morning?
   B: Yes, I .... I .... (have) some on my way to work.

B **PAIR WORK** Ask and answer the questions in part A. Give your own information.

5 LISTENING *What are they talking about?*

▶ Listen to six people ask questions about food and drink in a restaurant. Check (✓) the item that each person is talking about.

1. ☐ water   2. ☐ a meal   3. ☐ soup   4. ☐ coffee   5. ☐ cake   6. ☐ the check
   ☐ bread   ☐ a plate   ☐ pasta   ☐ meat   ☐ coffee   ☐ the menu

6 SPEAKING Tell me more!

PAIR WORK Ask your partner these questions and four
more of your own. Then ask follow-up questions.

Have you ever drunk fresh coconut juice?
Have you ever been to a vegetarian restaurant?
Have you ever had an unusual ice-cream flavor?
Have you ever eaten something you didn't like?

A: Have you ever drunk fresh coconut juice?
B: Yes, I have.
A: Did you like it?
B: Yes, I did. Actually, I ordered a second one!

7 INTERCHANGE 4 Is that so?

Find out some interesting facts about your classmates. Go to Interchange 4 on page 117.

8 WORD POWER Cooking methods

A How do you cook the foods below? Check (✓) the methods that are
most common in your country. Then compare with a partner.

bake   **boil**   **fry**   **grill**   **roast**   **steam**

Methods	Foods								
	fish	shrimp	eggs	chicken	beef	potatoes	onions	eggplant	bananas
bake	☐	☐	☐	☐	☐	☐	☐	☐	☐
boil	☐	☐	☐	☐	☐	☐	☐	☐	☐
fry	☐	☐	☐	☐	☐	☐	☐	☐	☐
grill	☐	☐	☐	☐	☐	☐	☐	☐	☐
roast	☐	☐	☐	☐	☐	☐	☐	☐	☐
steam	☐	☐	☐	☐	☐	☐	☐	☐	☐

B PAIR WORK What's your favorite way to cook or eat the foods in part A?

A: Have you ever steamed fish?
B: No, I haven't. I prefer to bake it.

9 *PERSPECTIVES* *Family cookbook*

A ▶ Listen to this recipe for Elvis Presley's favorite sandwich. Do you think this is a healthy snack?

S A N D W I C H E S

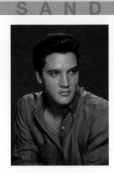

Peanut butter and banana

3 tablespoons peanut butter
1 banana, mashed
2 slices of bread
2 tablespoons butter, melted

First, mix the peanut butter and mashed banana together. Then lightly toast the slices of bread. Next, spread the peanut butter and banana mixture on the toast.

After that, close the sandwich and put it in a pan with melted butter. Finally, fry the bread until it's brown on both sides.

S A N D W I C H E S

B PAIR WORK Look at the steps in the recipe again. Number the pictures from 1 to 5. Would you like to try Elvis's specialty?

10 *GRAMMAR FOCUS*

> ### Sequence adverbs ▶
>
> **First**, mix the peanut butter and banana together.
> **Then** toast the slices of bread.
> **Next**, spread the mixture on the toast.
> **After that**, put the sandwich in a pan with butter.
> **Finally**, fry the sandwich until it's brown on both sides.

A Here's a recipe for grilled kebabs. Look at the pictures and number the steps from 1 to 5. Then add a sequence adverb to each step.

- ☐ .... put the meat and vegetables on the skewers.
- ☐ 1 ...First..... put charcoal in the grill and light it.
- ☐ .... take the kebabs off the grill and enjoy!
- ☐ .... put the kebabs on the grill and cook for 10 to 15 minutes, turning them over from time to time.
- ☐ .... cut up some meat and vegetables. Marinate them for 20 minutes in your favorite sauce.

B PAIR WORK Cover the recipe and look only at the pictures. Explain each step of the recipe to your partner.

11 LISTENING *Tempting snacks*

A ▶ Listen to people explain how to make these snacks. Which snack are they talking about? Number the photos from 1 to 4. (There is one extra photo.)

☐ **a bagel** ☐ **cookies** ☐ **guacamole** ☐ **pizza** ☐ **popcorn**

B PAIR WORK Choose one of the snacks you just heard about. Tell your partner how to make it.

12 SPEAKING *My favorite snack*

GROUP WORK Discuss these questions.

What's your favorite snack?
Is it easy to make?
What's in it?
When do you eat it?
How often do you eat it?
How healthy is it?

"My favorite snack is ramen. It's very easy to make. First, . . ."

13 WRITING *A recipe*

A Read this recipe. Is this an easy recipe to make?

Spicy Salsa

half an onion	2 chili peppers
5 tomatoes	a small bunch of cilantro
salt and pepper	1 lemon

First, chop the onion, chili peppers, tomatoes, and cilantro. Put in a bowl. Next, add salt and pepper. Then squeeze some fresh lemon juice in the bowl. After that, mix everything together and refrigerate for one hour. Enjoy with tortilla chips.

B Now think of something you know how to make. First, write down the things you need. Then describe how to make it.

C GROUP WORK Read and discuss each recipe. Then choose one to share with the class. Explain why you chose it.

Search [   ] Go

SIGN IN   HOME   RESEARCH   NEWSLETTER   ABOUT US

FOOD & MOOD

🐦 Follow   f Share 5

Skim the article. Then check (✓) the main idea.
☐ **Certain foods cause stress and depression.** ☐ **Certain foods affect the way we feel.**

We often eat to calm down or cheer up when we're feeling stressed or depressed. Now new research suggests there's a reason: Food changes our brain chemistry. These changes powerfully influence our moods. But can certain foods really make us feel better? Nutrition experts say yes. But what should we eat, and what should we avoid? Here are the foods that work the best, as well as those that can make a bad day worse.

To Outsmart Stress

What's good? Recent research suggests that foods that are high in carbohydrates, such as bread, rice, and pasta, can help you calm down. Researchers say that carbohydrates cause the brain to release a chemical called serotonin. Serotonin makes you feel better.

What's bad? Many people drink coffee when they feel stress. The warmth is soothing, and the caffeine in coffee might help you think more clearly. But if you drink too much, you may become even more anxious and irritable.

To Soothe the Blues

What's good? Introduce more lean meat, chicken, seafood, and whole grains into your diet. These foods have a lot of selenium. Selenium is a mineral that helps people feel more relaxed and happy. You can also try eating a Brazil nut every day. One Brazil nut contains a lot of selenium.

What's bad? When they're feeling low, many people turn to comfort foods – or foods that make them feel happy or secure. These often include things like sweet desserts. A chocolate bar may make you feel better at first, but within an hour you may feel worse than you did before.

A Read the article. The sentences below are false. Correct each sentence to make it true.

1. We often eat when we feel calm.
2. You should drink coffee to relieve stress.
3. Foods like chicken and seafood are high in carbohydrates.
4. Carbohydrates cause the brain to release selenium.
5. Serotonin makes you feel more anxious and irritable.
6. People usually eat comfort foods when they're feeling happy.
7. Brazil nuts don't contain much selenium.
8. Chocolate will make you feel better.

B PAIR WORK What foods do you eat to feel better? After reading the article, which of the suggestions will you follow?

I've never heard of that! ▪ 27

Units 3–4 Progress check

SELF-ASSESSMENT

How well can you do these things? Check (✓) the boxes.

I can	Very well	OK	A little
Describe a house or an apartment (Ex. 1)	☐	☐	☐
Express opinions about houses or apartments; agree and disagree (Ex. 1)	☐	☐	☐
Understand and express personal wishes (Ex. 2)	☐	☐	☐
Ask and answer questions about past actions and personal experiences (Ex. 3)	☐	☐	☐
Describe recipes (Ex. 4)	☐	☐	☐

1 SPEAKING Apartment ads

A PAIR WORK Use the topics in the box to write an ad for an apartment.
Use this ad as a model. Make the apartment sound as good as possible.

Quiet, Private Apartment
Small, but very comfortable, with many windows;
located downtown; convenient to stores; 1 bedroom,
1 bathroom; 1-car garage; $850 a month!

age	windows	parking
size	bathroom(s)	cost
location	bedroom(s)	noise

B GROUP WORK Join another pair. Evaluate and compare the apartments.
Which would you prefer to rent? Why?

A: There aren't enough bedrooms in your apartment.
B: But it's convenient.
C: Yes, but our apartment is just as convenient!

2 LISTENING I really need a change!

A ⊙ Listen to three people talk about things they wish they could change.
Check (✓) the topic each person is talking about.

1. ☐ free time   ☐ school   ....
2. ☐ skills   ☐ hobbies   ....
3. ☐ family   ☐ travel   ....

B ⊙ Listen again. Write one change each person would like to make.

C GROUP WORK Use the topics in part A to express some wishes.
How can you make the wishes come true? Offer suggestions.

28

3 SURVEY Food experiences

A Complete the survey with your food opinions and experiences.
Then use your information to write questions.

Me	Name
1. I've eaten .... I liked it. Have you ever eaten .... ? Did you like it?	....
2. I've eaten .... I hated it. .... ? .... ?	....
3. I've never tried .... But I want to.	....
4. I've been to the restaurant .... I enjoyed it.	....
5. I've made .... for my friends. They loved it.	....

B **CLASS ACTIVITY** Go around the class and ask your
questions. Find people who have the same opinions
and experiences. Write a classmate's name only once.

A: Have you ever eaten peanut butter?
B: Yes, I have.
A: Did you like it?
B: No, not really.

4 ROLE PLAY Iron Chef

GROUP WORK Work in groups of four. Two students are the
judges. Two students are the chefs.

Judges: Make a list of three ingredients for the chefs
to use. You will decide which chef creates the
best recipe.

Chefs: Think of a recipe using the three ingredients
the judges give you and other basic ingredients.
Name the recipe and describe how to make it.

"My recipe is called . . . . To make it,
first . . . . Then . . . . Next, . . . "

Change roles and try the role play again.

Iron Chef, **a TV
cooking competition**

WHAT'S NEXT?

Look at your Self-assessment again. Do you need to review anything?

5 Going places

What do you like to do on vacation?

Take a fun trip	Discover something new	Stay home	Enjoy nature

- travel in my country
- visit a foreign country

- visit museums
- go to a music festival

- hang out with friends
- watch movies

- go fishing
- relax at the beach

Source: Based on information from *U.S. News and World Report; American Demographics*

Which activities do you like to do on vacation? Check (✓) the activities.
Which activities did you do on your last vacation?
Make a list of other activities you like to do on vacation. Then compare with a partner.

2 CONVERSATION *What are you going to do?*

A ▶ Listen and practice.

Julia: I'm so excited! We have two weeks off!
What are you going to do?

Nancy: I'm not sure. I guess I'll just stay home.
Maybe I'll hang out with my friends and watch
some movies. What about you? Any plans?

Julia: Yeah, I'm going to relax at the beach with my
cousin. We're going to go surfing every day.
And my cousin likes to fish, so maybe
we'll go fishing one day.

Nancy: Sounds like fun.

Julia: Say, why don't you come with us?

Nancy: Do you mean it? I'd love to! I'll bring my surfboard!

Julia: That's great! The more the merrier!

B ▶ Listen to the rest of the conversation. Where
are they going to stay? How will they get there?

Future with be going to and will ▶

Use **be going to** + verb for plans you've decided on.	Use **will** + verb for possible plans before you've made a decision.
What **are** you **going to do**?	What **are** you **going to do**?
I**'m going to relax** at the beach.	I'm not sure. I **guess** I**'ll** just **stay** home.
We**'re going to go** surfing every day.	**Maybe** I**'ll watch** some movies.
I**'m** not **going to do** anything special.	I don't know. I **think** I**'ll go** camping.
	I **probably won't go** anywhere.

A Complete the conversation with appropriate forms of *be going to* or *will*. Then compare with a partner.

A: Have you made any vacation plans?

B: Well, I've decided on one thing –
I .... go camping.

A: That's great! For how long?

B: I .... be away for a week.
I only have five days of vacation.

A: So, when are you leaving?

B: I'm not sure. I .... probably leave
around the end of May.

A: And where .... you .... go?

B: I haven't thought about that yet. I guess
I .... go to one of the national parks.

A: That sounds like fun.

B: Yeah. Maybe I .... go
hiking and do some fishing.

A: .... you .... rent a camper?

B: I'm not sure. Actually, I probably ....
rent a camper – it's too expensive.

A: .... you .... go with anyone?

B: No. I need some time alone.
I .... travel by myself.

B Have you thought about your next vacation? Write answers to these questions. (If you already have plans, use *be going to*. If you don't have fixed plans, use *will*.)

1. How are you going to spend your next vacation?
2. Where are you going to go?
3. When are you going to take your vacation?
4. How long are you going to be on vacation?
5. Is anyone going to travel with you?

> I'm going to spend my next vacation . . .
> OR
> I'm not sure. Maybe I'll . . .

C **GROUP WORK** Take turns telling the group about your vacation plans.
Use your information from part B.

WORD POWER *Travel planning*

A Complete the chart. Then add one more word to each category.

ATM card   cash   hiking boots   plane ticket   suitcase
backpack   credit card   medication   sandals   swimsuit
carry-on bag   first–aid kit passport   student ID   vaccination

Clothing	Money	Health	Documents	Luggage
....	....	....	....	....
....	....	....	....	....
....	....	....	....	....
....	....	....	....	....

B **PAIR WORK** What are the five most important items you need for these vacations?

a hiking trip   a rafting trip   a trip to a foreign country

INTERCHANGE 5 *Fun vacations*

Decide between two vacations. Student A, go to Interchange 5A on page 118;
Student B, go to Interchange 5B on page 120.

PERSPECTIVES *Travel advice*

A Listen to these pieces of advice from experienced travelers.
What topic is each person talking about?

"You should tell the driver where you're going before you get on. And you have to have exact change for the fare."

"In most countries, you don't have to have an international driver's license, but you must have a license from your own country. You also need to be 21 or over."

"You should try some of the local specialties, but you'd better avoid the stalls on the street."

"You ought to pack a first-aid kit and any medication you need. You shouldn't drink water from the tap."

"When you fly, you should keep important things in your carry-on bag, such as your medication and credit cards. You shouldn't pack them in your checked luggage."

"You ought to keep a copy of your credit card numbers at the hotel. And you shouldn't carry a lot of cash when you go out."

B **PAIR WORK** Look at the advice again. Do you think this is all good advice? Why or why not?

GRAMMAR FOCUS

Modals for necessity and suggestion ▶

Describing necessity
You **must** have a driver's license.
You **need to** be 21 or over.
You **have to** get a passport.
You **don't have to** get vaccinations.

Giving suggestions
You**'d better** avoid the stalls on the street.
You **ought to** pack a first-aid kit.
You **should** try some local specialties.
You **shouldn't** carry a lot of cash.

A Choose the best advice for someone who is going on vacation. Then compare with a partner.

1. You .... make hotel reservations in advance. It might be difficult to find a room after you get there. (have to / 'd better)
2. You .... carry identification with you. It's the law! (must / should)
3. You .... buy a round-trip plane ticket because it's cheaper. (must / should)
4. You .... pack too many clothes. You won't have room to bring back any gifts. (don't have to / shouldn't)
5. You .... check out of most hotel rooms by noon if you don't want to pay for another night. (need to / ought to)
6. You .... buy a new suitcase because your old one is getting shabby. (have to / ought to)

B **PAIR WORK** Imagine you're going to travel abroad. Take turns giving each other advice.

"You must get the necessary vaccinations."

1. You . . . get the necessary vaccinations.
2. You . . . take your ATM card with you.
3. You . . . take your student ID. It might get you discounts.
4. You . . . forget to pack your camera.
5. You . . . have a visa to enter some foreign countries.
6. You . . . change money before you go. You can do it when you arrive.

C **GROUP WORK** What advice would you give someone who is going to study English abroad? Report your best ideas to the class.

8 PRONUNCIATION *Linked sounds with /w/ and /y/*

▶ Listen and practice. Notice how some words are linked by a /w/ sound, and other words are linked by a /y/ sound.

/w/
You should know about local conditions.

/y/
You shouldn't carry a lot of cash.

/w/
You ought to do it right away.

/y/
You must be at least 21 years old.

9 LISTENING *Tourist tips*

A ▶ Listen to an interview with a spokeswoman from the New York City Visitors Center. Check (✓) the four topics she discusses.

☐ eating out ☐ history ☐ money ☐ planning a trip ☐ safety ☐ tours

B ▶ Listen again. For each topic, write one piece of advice she gives.

10 WRITING *Travel suggestions*

A Imagine someone is going to visit your town, city, or country. Write a letter giving some suggestions for sightseeing activities.

> Dear Josh,
>
> I'm so glad you're going to visit Santiago! As you know, Santiago is a very old and beautiful city, so you should bring your camera. Also, you ought to bring some good shoes because we're going to walk a lot. It will be warm, so you don't have to pack . . .

B PAIR WORK Exchange letters. Is there anything else the visitor needs to know about (food, money, business hours, etc.)?

11 DISCUSSION *Dream vacation*

A PAIR WORK You just won a free 30-day trip around the world. Discuss the following questions.

When will you leave and return?
Which direction will you go (east or west)?
Where will you choose to stop? Why?
How will you get from place to place?
How long will you stay in each place?

B PAIR WORK What do you need to do before you go? Discuss these topics.

reservations	documents	vaccinations
money	shopping	packing

A: We should make a hotel reservation for the first night.
B: Yes, and I think we ought to buy some guidebooks.

Volunteer Travel – A vacation with a difference

Check (✓) the statements you think are true. Then scan the article to check your answers.
- *Volunteer travelers don't receive money for their work.*
- *Volunteer travel is only for young people.*

For her vacation each year, Allie Lebrun goes volunteer traveling. In a recent interview with *Volunteer Magazine,* she talked about volunteer vacations.

VM: --

AL: It's like an exchange program. People find a program in a country they'd like to visit. In exchange for food and accommodations, they work. In other words, they don't get a salary. The idea is that volunteers can learn about real people in other countries. Vacationers who stay in hotels often don't learn much about the local people and culture.

VM: --

AL: Many of the jobs are on small farms. Farmers often need volunteers to harvest crops. I've harvested vegetables and fruit – including nuts and olives! Some volunteers work with animals, such as milking cows or goats. That's an interesting experience, I can tell you! And sometimes farmers want volunteers to do things like build stone walls. There are lots of possibilities.

VM: --

AL: Anyone! Many volunteers are fairly young. The work can be hard, so a volunteer needs to be fit. But, actually, age isn't important. I've worked with people in their seventies and even eighties!

VM: --

AL: Just about anywhere in the world! I've volunteered in Italy, Morocco, Indonesia, and several countries in Latin America.

VM: --

AL: Oh, that's easy! Just go online. Do a search for "volunteer travel" or "volunteer vacations." You'll find lots of websites with information about opportunities for volunteering. Maybe there's a program in a country you've always wanted to visit!

A Read the article. Then write these questions in the appropriate place.

1. What kinds of work can volunteers do?
2. Where can people volunteer to work?
3. Who can volunteer?

4. And finally, how can someone find out about volunteer travel opportunities?
5. What is volunteer traveling?

B Complete the summary with information from the article.

Allie Lebrun goes .... every year. She says that volunteers get .... in exchange for .... Volunteers often work on .... and harvest .... To volunteer, you have to be fit, but age .... You can work .... in the world. To find places to work, ... There are .... with information about volunteer traveling.

C GROUP WORK Would you like to volunteer travel? Where would you like to go? What kind of work would you like to do? Why?

6 OK. No problem!

1 SNAPSHOT

Common Complaints of Families with Teenagers

MY KIDS...
- [ ] don't help around the house
- [ ] are always texting their friends
- [ ] never listen to us
- [ ] eat too much junk food
- [ ] leave everything until the last minute

MY PARENTS...
- [ ] embarrass me in front of my friends
- [ ] don't respect my privacy
- [ ] criticize my taste in music
- [ ] nag me to clean up my room
- [ ] won't let me make my own decisions

Sources: Based on interviews with parents and teenagers

Which complaints seem reasonable? Which ones seem unreasonable? Why?
Check (✓) a complaint you have about a family member.
What other complaints do people sometimes have about family members?

2 CONVERSATION *Turn down the TV!*

A ▶ Listen and practice.

Mr. Field: Jason . . . Jason! Turn down the TV, please.
Jason: Oh, but this is my favorite program!
Mr. Field: I know. But it's very loud.
Jason: OK. I'll turn it down.
Mr. Field: That's better. Thanks.
Mrs. Field: Lisa, please pick up your things. They're all over the floor.
Lisa: In a minute, Mom. I'm on the phone.
Mrs. Field: All right. But do it as soon as you hang up.
Lisa: OK. No problem!
Mrs. Field: Were we like this when we were kids?
Mr. Field: Definitely!

B ▶ Listen to the rest of the conversation. What complaints do Jason and Lisa have about their parents?

GRAMMAR FOCUS

Two-part verbs; will *for responding to requests* ▶

With nouns	With pronouns	Requests and responses
Turn down the TV.	**Turn it** down.	Please turn down the music.
Turn the TV **down**.	(NOT: ~~Turn down it.~~)	OK. I'**ll** turn it down.
Pick up your things.	**Pick** them **up**.	Pick up your clothes, please.
Pick your things **up**.	(NOT: ~~Pick up them.~~)	All right. I'**ll** pick them up.

A Complete the requests with these words. Then compare with a partner.

the books

the toys

the music

your jacket

the TV

your boots

the yard

the lights

the trash

the cat

1. Pick up ....the toys........ , please.
2. Turn .... off, please.
3. Clean .... up, please.
4. Please put .... away.
5. Please turn down ....

6. Please take off ....
7. Hang .... up, please.
8. Please take out ....
9. Please let .... out.
10. Turn on .... , please.

B PAIR WORK Take turns making the requests above. Respond with pronouns.

A: Pick up the toys, please.
B: No problem. I'll pick them up.

4 PRONUNCIATION Stress in two-part verbs

A ▶ Listen and practice. Both words in a two-part verb receive equal stress.

●	●	○	●		●	○	●	●		●	○	●
Pick	up	the	toys.		Pick	the	toys	up.		Pick	them	up.
Turn	off	the	light.		Turn	the	light	off.		Turn	it	off.

B Write four more requests using the verbs in Exercise 3.
Then practice with a partner. Pay attention to stress.

WORD POWER *Household chores*

A Find a phrase that is usually paired with each two-part verb. (Some phrases go with more than one verb.) Then add one more phrase for each verb.

the garbage   the magazines   the microwave   your coat
the groceries   the mess   the towels   your laptop

clean up	....	....	take out	....	....
hang up	....	....	throw out	....	....
pick up	....	....	turn off	....	....
put away	....	....	turn on	....	....

B What requests can you make in each of these rooms? Write four requests and four excuses. Use two-part verbs.

the kitchen   the living room
the bathroom   the bedroom

C **PAIR WORK** Take turns making the requests you wrote in part B. Respond by giving an excuse.

A: Kim, please hang up the coat you left in the living room.
B: Sorry, I can't hang it up right now. I need to take the cat out for a walk.

 LISTENING *Family life*

A  Listen to the results of a survey about family life. Answer each question with men (**M**), women (**W**), boys (**B**), or girls (**G**).

Who is the messiest person in the house? ....
Who does most of the work in the kitchen? ....
Who usually takes out the garbage? ....
Who worries most about expenses? ....

B Listen again. According to the survey, what specific chores do men, women, boys, and girls usually do? Take notes.

C **GROUP WORK** Discuss the questions in parts A and B. Who does these things in your family?

A Match the sentences. Then listen and check your answers. Are all the requests reasonable?

1. "Could you please tell me the next time you have a party? ....
2. "Can you turn the music down, please? ....
3. "Would you mind closing the door behind you and making sure it locks? ....
4. "Would you please tell your guests to use the visitor parking spaces? ....
5. "Would you mind not putting your garbage in the hallway? ....

a. It's not very pleasant to see when I walk by."
b. We don't want strangers to enter the building."
c. The walls are really thin, so the sound goes through to my apartment."
d. A lot of cars have been using my space recently."
e. I'd like to make sure I'm not at home."

B Look at the requests again. Have you ever made similar requests? Has anyone ever asked you to do similar things?

8 **GRAMMAR FOCUS**

> ### Requests with modals and Would you mind . . . ?
>
> | **Modal + simple form of verb** | **Would you mind . . . + gerund** |
> |---|---|
> | **Can** you **turn** the music **down**? | **Would you mind turning** the music **down**? |
> | **Could** you **close** the door, please? | **Would you mind closing** the door, please? |
> | **Would** you please **take** your garbage **out**? | **Would you mind not putting** your garbage here? |

A Match the requests in column A with the appropriate responses in column B. Then compare with a partner and practice them. (More than one answer may be possible.)

A
1. Could you lend me twenty dollars? ....
2. Can you make me a sandwich? ....
3. Can you help me with my homework? ....
4. Would you mind not sitting here? ....
5. Would you please turn down the TV? ....
6. Would you mind speaking more quietly? ....

B
a. Sorry. We didn't know we were so loud.
b. Sure. Do you want anything to drink?
c. Sorry. I didn't realize this seat was taken.
d. I'm sorry, I can't. I don't have any cash.
e. I'm really sorry, but I'm busy.
f. Sure, no problem. I'd be glad to.

B **PAIR WORK** Take turns making the requests in part A. Give your own responses.

C **CLASS ACTIVITY** Think of five unusual requests. Go around the class and make your requests. How many people accept? How many refuse?

A: Would you please sing a song for me?
B: Oh, I'm sorry. I'm a terrible singer.

9 SPEAKING *Apologies*

A Think of three complaints you have about your neighbors. Write three requests you want to make. Choose from these topics or use ideas of your own.

garbage   guests   noise   parking   pets   security

B **PAIR WORK** Take turns making your requests. The "neighbor" should apologize by giving an excuse, admitting a mistake, or making an offer or a promise.

A: Would you mind not putting your garbage in the hallway?
B: Oh, I'm sorry. I didn't realize it bothered you.

different ways to apologize	
give an excuse	"I'm sorry. I didn't realize . . ."
admit a mistake	"I forgot I left it there."
make an offer	"I'll take it out right now."
make a promise	"I promise I'll . . . / I'll make sure to . . ."

10 INTERCHANGE 6 *That's no excuse!*

How good are you at apologizing? Go to Interchange 6 on page 119.

11 WRITING *A set of guidelines*

A **PAIR WORK** Imagine that you live in a large apartment building. Use complaints from Exercise 9 and your own ideas to write a set of six guidelines.

The Riverview Apartments

Please read the following tenant association guidelines. Feel free to contact Joseph (#205) or Tina (#634) if you have any questions.

1. Don't park bicycles on the sidewalk. Everyone must use the bike rack.

2. Can everyone please keep the laundry room clean? Please pick up after yourself!

3. Would you mind not picking the flowers in the garden? They're for everyone's enjoyment.

B **GROUP WORK** Take turns reading your guidelines aloud. What is the best new guideline? the worst one?

How to Ask for a Favor

Read the headings in the article. Can you think of other good advice when asking for a favor?

We all have to ask for favors sometimes. But it can be a difficult thing to do – even when you ask a good friend. So how can you ask a favor and be reasonably sure to get a positive response? Here are some suggestions.

Mike, would you mind doing me a favor?

Choose your words carefully

How do people respond to requests like this one: "Hey, Mike, lend me your car!"? They probably refuse. How can you avoid this problem? Choose your words carefully! For example, say, "Mike, would you mind doing me a favor?" Mike will probably respond like this: "Maybe. What do you need?" Now you have his attention and can explain the situation. People are more likely to agree to help you when they know the whole story.

Be a nice person

When you ask someone for a favor, you're really asking the person to go out of his or her way to help you. Show the person that you understand he or she is doing something especially nice for you. If people think you're pleasant, they're more likely to want to help. Thank them sincerely when they help you. And, of course, a smile goes a long way.

Give and take

If someone agrees to do you a favor, allow the person to choose when he or she helps you. Be respectful of the other person's time, and try not to ask for too much. If someone refuses your request, you should accept the answer politely. Don't make a habit of asking for favors, and always make sure you're ready to do someone a favor in return. Reciprocate. It's just a matter of giving and taking.

A Read the article. Find the words in *italics* below in the article. Then match each word with its meaning.

.... 1. *especially*   a. give in return
.... 2. *pleasant*   b. say no
.... 3. *sincerely*   c. friendly
.... 4. *refuse*   d. more than usually
.... 5. *avoid*   e. honestly
.... 6. *reciprocate*   f. stop from happening

B Check (✓) the questions that the article answers. Then find sentences in the article that support your answers.

☐ 1. Why is it easy to ask for a favor?
☐ 2. How can you show people you're nice?
☐ 3. How can you avoid people asking for favors?
☐ 4. What do you do when someone refuses?
☐ 5. Why is it not a good idea to ask for a lot of favors?

C **PAIR WORK** Think about a favor you asked someone to do. Did the person do it? Then think about a favor someone asked you to do. Did you do it? Why or why not?

Units 5–6 Progress check

SELF-ASSESSMENT

How well can you do these things? Check (✓) the boxes.

I can	Very well	OK	A little
Understand descriptions of people's plans (Ex. 1)	☐	☐	☐
Ask and answer questions about personal plans (Ex. 2)	☐	☐	☐
Give travel advice (Ex. 2)	☐	☐	☐
Make and respond to practical requests (Ex. 3, 4)	☐	☐	☐
Apologize and give excuses (Ex. 3, 4)	☐	☐	☐

1 LISTENING *Summer plans*

A ▶ Listen to Judy, Paul, and Brenda describe their summer plans.
What is each person going to do?

	Summer plans	Reason
1. Judy	....	....
2. Paul	....	....
3. Brenda	....	....

B ▶ Listen again. What is the reason for each person's choice?

2 DISCUSSION *Planning a vacation*

A GROUP WORK Imagine you are going to go on vacation.
Take turns asking and answering these questions.

A: **Where are you going to go on your next vacation?**
B: I'm going to go to Utah.
A: **What are you going to do?**
B: I'm going to go camping and hiking.
Maybe I'll try rock climbing.
A: **Why did you choose that?**
B: Well, I really enjoy nature. And I want to do
something different!

B GROUP WORK What should each person do to prepare
for his or her vacation? Give each other advice.

3 ROLE PLAY *Excuses, excuses!*

Student A: Your partner was supposed to do some things, but didn't. Look at the pictures and make a request about each one.

Student B: You were supposed to do some things, but didn't. Listen to your partner's requests. Apologize and either agree to the request or give an excuse.

A: You left the towels on the floor. Please hang them up.
B: I'm sorry. I forgot about them. I'll hang them up right now.

Change roles and try the role play again.

4 GAME *Could you do me a favor?*

A Write three requests on separate cards. Put an *X* on the back of two of the cards.

| Can you cook dinner tonight? | Could you get me a cup of coffee? | Would you mind closing the window? |

B CLASS ACTIVITY Shuffle all the cards together. Take three new cards.

Go around the class and take turns making requests with the cards. Hold up each card so your classmate can see the back.

When answering:
X on the back = refuse the request and give an excuse
No *X* = agree to the request

Can you cook dinner tonight?

I'm sorry, I can't. I'm . . .

WHAT'S NEXT?

Look at your Self-assessment again. Do you need to review anything?

7 What's this for?

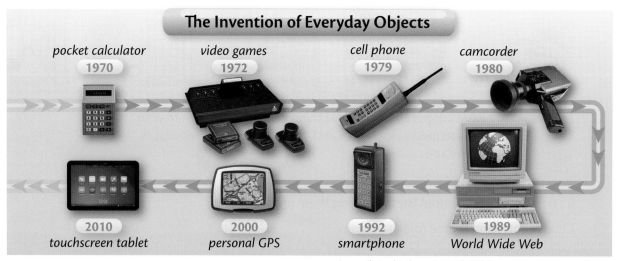

The Invention of Everyday Objects

pocket calculator	video games	cell phone	camcorder
1970	1972	1979	1980

2010	2000	1992	1989
touchscreen tablet	personal GPS	smartphone	World Wide Web

Sources: *The People's Almanac Presents the 20th Century*; www.about.com; www.ehow.com

Circle the things that you use every day or almost every day.
Which invention do you think is the most important? the least important?
What are some other things you use every day?

2 PERSPECTIVES *Computer usage*

A How do you use a computer? Listen and respond to the statements.

Rate Your Computer Usage

I use a computer . . .	Often	Sometimes	Hardly ever	Never
to send emails	☐	☐	☐	☐
for watching movies	☐	☐	☐	☐
to play games	☐	☐	☐	☐
to shop online	☐	☐	☐	☐
for doing school assignments	☐	☐	☐	☐
to learn languages	☐	☐	☐	☐
for video chatting	☐	☐	☐	☐
to check the weather	☐	☐	☐	☐
to read the news	☐	☐	☐	☐
for downloading music	☐	☐	☐	☐

B **PAIR WORK** Compare your answers. Are your answers similar or different?

3 GRAMMAR FOCUS

Infinitives and gerunds for uses and purposes ▶

Infinitives	Gerunds
I use my computer **to send** emails.	I use my computer **for sending** emails.
Some people use computers **to play** games.	Some people use computers **for playing** games.
Computers are often used **to watch** movies.	Computers are often used **for watching** movies.

A PAIR WORK What do you know about this technology? Complete the sentences in column A with information from column B. Use infinitives and gerunds. (More than one combination is possible.)

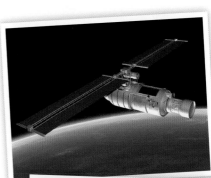

A
1. Satellites are used . . .
2. Robots are sometimes used . . .
3. You can use a cell phone . . .
4. People use the Internet . . .
5. A GPS device is used . . .
6. A tablet computer can be used . . .

B
study the world's weather
perform dangerous tasks
read e-books
transmit telephone calls
send text messages
get directions
make travel reservations
transmit TV shows
shop online

> Satellites are used to study the world's weather.
> Satellites are used for studying the world's weather.

B GROUP WORK Think of three more items of technology. Then talk about possible uses for each one.

"You can use an MP3 player to listen to podcasts."

4 PRONUNCIATION Syllable stress

A ▶ Listen and practice. Notice which syllable has the main stress.

⬤ ○ ○	○ ⬤ ○	○ ○ ⬤
satellite	invention	CD-ROM
Internet	assignment	engineer
messages	computer	entertain
....	....	....
....	....	....

B ▶ Where is the stress in these words? Add them to the columns in part A. Then listen and check.

directions   DVD   media   telephone   transmission   understand

What's this for? ▪ 45

5 WORD POWER The world of computers

A Complete the chart with words and phrases from the list. Add one more to each category. Then compare with a partner.

✓ browse websites	cut and paste	geek	monitor
computer whiz	drag and drop	hacker	mouse
create a slideshow	edit a video	highlight text	open a file
create song playlists	flash drive	keyboard	technophile

People who are "into" computers	Type of computer hardware	Fun things to do with a computer	Things to do with a mouse
		browse websites	

B GROUP WORK Discuss how computers have changed our lives. Ask and answer questions like these:

How do computers make your life easier? more difficult?
How do they affect the way you spend your free time?
How do they influence the kinds of jobs people have?
What kinds of problems do they cause?
Do you know anyone who is a computer whiz?
Are hackers a problem where you live?

6 LISTENING Off-line – and proud of it!

A ▶ Guess the answers to the questions below. Then listen to a radio program about the Internet and check your answers.

What percentage of the U.S. population never uses the Internet? What kinds of people don't use the Internet?

B ▶ Listen to the rest of the program. Then answer these questions.

What does the term "net evaders" mean?
What are "Internet dropouts"?
Why do some people become Internet dropouts?

7 CONVERSATION *I give up!*

A ▶ Listen and practice.

Terry: I give up! I can't figure this out.

Rachel: What's wrong?

Terry: I'm trying to create a song playlist for my party on Saturday.

Rachel: I can help. It's really easy. First, choose "New Playlist" from the menu.

Terry: Here? Oh, I see.

Rachel: Now type in the name of your playlist. Then go to your song file and choose the ones you want.

Terry: But how do I choose the songs?

Rachel: Just drag them to the playlist. Be sure to press these keys to highlight more than one song.

Terry: That *was* easy. Thanks! So are you coming on Saturday?

Rachel: Of course. But don't forget to include my favorite songs on your playlist, OK?

B ▶ Listen to the rest of the conversation. What else does Terry want help with?

8 GRAMMAR FOCUS

Imperatives and infinitives for giving suggestions ▶

Be sure to press these keys.
Make sure to save your work.
Remember to back up your files.

Don't forget to include my favorite songs.
Try not to be late for the party.

A Look at these suggestions. Which ones refer to (a) an alarm system? (b) a smartphone? (c) a laptop? (More than one answer is sometimes possible.)

1. Try to keep it closed to protect the screen. ....
2. Don't forget to write down your secret code. ....
3. Remember to turn it off as soon as you come in the door. ....
4. Try not to get it wet or the keys may get stuck. ....
5. Make sure to set it each time you leave home. ....
6. Remember to recharge the battery before it dies. ....
7. Be sure to turn it off before bed or a call may wake you up. ....
8. Make sure to keep the software up to date. ....

B GROUP WORK Take turns giving other suggestions for using the items in part A. Use these phrases.

Make sure to . . .	Try to . . .	Remember to . . .
Be sure not to . . .	Try not to . . .	Don't forget to . . .

9 LISTENING Good suggestions

A ▶ Listen to people give suggestions about three of these things.
Number them 1, 2, and 3. (There are two extra things.)

MP4 player

ATM card

GPS system

video camera

flash drive

B ▶ Listen again. Write two suggestions you hear for each thing. Then compare
with a partner.

1. ....
2. ....
3. ....

C PAIR WORK What do you know about the two other things in part A?
What suggestions can you give about them?

10 INTERCHANGE 7 Talk radio

Give callers to a radio program some advice. Go to Interchange 7 on page 121.

11 WRITING An email

A Imagine you're sick today and can't go to class. A classmate has agreed to
help you. Think of three things you need him or her to do for you. Then write
an email with instructions.

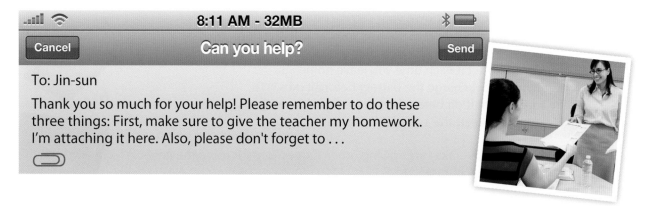

B GROUP WORK Take turns reading your emails aloud. Do you have similar favors?

Modern-Day Treasure Hunters

Scan the article. What is geocaching? Who enjoys it? Why?

Geocaching is a game played worldwide – even though it only began in 2000! *Geo* is from the word *geography,* and *caching* (pronounced "cashing") means hiding a container with "treasure" inside. The purpose of geocaching is to use GPS technology to find a hidden cache – some people call it a high-tech treasure-hunting game. Technophiles love it because you need technology. Hikers love it because you may have to walk a long way. And looking for treasure is fun, so it's also great for children.

It isn't difficult to become a geocacher. First, buy a small handheld GPS device. Next, search online for a geocaching website and choose a cache to look for. Some caches are in beautiful locations, such as river valleys, mountains, or beaches. For each cache, websites list coordinates – numbers that give an exact geographical position (for example, 48°51.29' N, 02°17.40' E is the Eiffel Tower in Paris). Input the coordinates for your cache into your GPS device, and you're ready to go!

Your GPS device will identify the exact location of your cache. That's the easy part. The hard part comes after you get to the location – finding the cache! Some caches are hidden under stones, in trees, or even in water. And what will you find in your cache? If you're looking for gold or diamonds, you'll be very disappointed. Most caches contain inexpensive things like books, toys, coins, or DVDs. There's also a logbook and pencil for you to record the date you found the cache and make comments. The real prize is the pleasure of saying, "I found it!"

Geocaching etiquette allows you to take whatever you want from the cache, but you must replace it with something of the same or higher value. Don't forget to bring some treasure for the next geocacher!

A Read the article. Check (✓) True or False for each statement. Then correct each false statement.

True	False		
☐	✓	1.	Geocaching is a new low-tech game. *It's a high-tech game.*
☐	☐	2.	Geocaching is popular in many countries.
☐	☐	3.	You need information from websites.
☐	☐	4.	Your GPS device gives you coordinates.
☐	☐	5.	Your GPS device finds cache locations for you.
☐	☐	6.	Caches contain pencils as well as treasure.
☐	☐	7.	Geocachers usually find gold.
☐	☐	8.	Geocaching is about giving and taking.

B **PAIR WORK** Have you ever been geocaching? If so, did you enjoy it? If not, would you like to try it? Why or why not?

8 Let's celebrate!

Chinese New Year
January or February
Chinese people celebrate the lunar new year with fireworks and lion dances.

Australia Day
January 26
Australians put on patriotic shows to celebrate their national day.

Children's Day
May 5
Japanese families put up colored streamers shaped like fish, in honor of their children.

Day of the Dead
November 2
Mexicans make playful skeleton sculptures and bake *pan de muerto* – bread of the dead.

Sources: *Reader's Digest Book of Facts*

Do you celebrate these or similar holidays in your country?
What other special days do you have?
What's your favorite holiday or festival?

2 WORD POWER *Collocations*

A Which word or phrase is not usually paired with each verb?
Put a line through it. Then compare with a partner.

1. **eat**	candy	rice cakes	~~juice~~
2. **give**	presents	relatives	candy
3. **go to**	decorations	a wedding	a party
4. **have**	a party	a beach	a meal
5. **play**	games	money	music
6. **send**	cards	flowers	a party
7. **visit**	relatives	food	friends
8. **watch**	a birthday	a parade	fireworks
9. **wear**	new clothes	a celebration	traditional clothes

B PAIR WORK Do you do any of the things in part A as part of a cultural or family celebration? When? Tell your partner.

50

A Listen to these comments about special days of the year. Match them to the correct pictures.

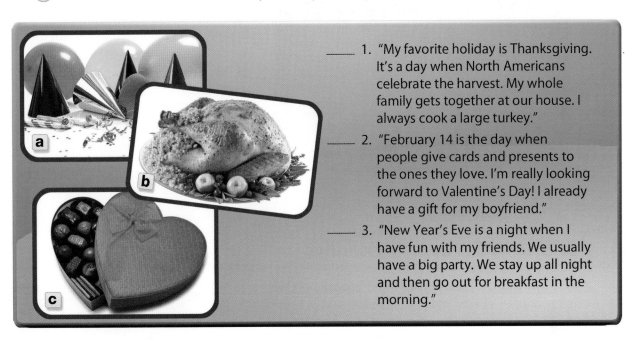

a

b

c

_____ 1. "My favorite holiday is Thanksgiving. It's a day when North Americans celebrate the harvest. My whole family gets together at our house. I always cook a large turkey."

_____ 2. "February 14 is the day when people give cards and presents to the ones they love. I'm really looking forward to Valentine's Day! I already have a gift for my boyfriend."

_____ 3. "New Year's Eve is a night when I have fun with my friends. We usually have a big party. We stay up all night and then go out for breakfast in the morning."

B **PAIR WORK** What do you like about each holiday in part A?

4 **GRAMMAR FOCUS**

> ### Relative clauses of time ▶
>
> | | |
> |---|---|
> | Thanksgiving is **a day** | **when** we celebrate the harvest. |
> | February 14 is **the day** | **when** people give cards to the ones they love. |
> | New Year's Eve is **a night** | **when** I have fun with my friends. |

A How much do you know about these times? Complete the sentences in column A with information from column B. Then compare with a partner.

A

1. New Year's Eve is a night when ....
2. April Fools' Day is a day when ....
3. Summer is a time when ....
4. Valentine's Day is a day when ....
5. Labor Day is a day when ....
6. Autumn is the season when ....

B

a. North Americans celebrate Thanksgiving.
b. students have a break from school.
c. people have parties with family and friends.
d. people in many countries honor workers.
e. people express their love to someone.
f. people sometimes play tricks on friends.

B Complete these sentences with your own information. Then compare with a partner.

Winter is the season . . .   Mother's Day is a day . . .
Birthdays are days . . .   July and August are the months . . .
Spring is the time of year . . .   A wedding anniversary is a time . . .

Let's celebrate! ▪ 51

5 LISTENING *Carnaval time*

Carnaval in Brazil

A ▶ Mike has just returned from Brazil. Listen to him talk about Carnaval. What was his favorite thing about it?

B ▶ Listen again and answer these questions.

What is Carnaval?
How long does it last?
When is it?
What is the samba?

6 SPEAKING *Favorite holidays*

A PAIR WORK Choose your three favorite holidays. Tell your partner why you like each one.

A: I really like Republic Day.
B: What do you like about it?
A: Well, it's a time when schools and offices are closed, and we have parades and fireworks.

B CLASS ACTIVITY Take a class vote. What are the most popular holidays in your class?

Republic Day in Turkey

Mid-Autumn Festival in Singapore

7 WRITING *An online entry*

A Write an entry for a travel website about a festival or celebration where you live. When is it? How do people celebrate it? What should a visitor see and do?

○○○ ◀   +

The annual fireworks festival in Yenshui, Taiwan, occurs on the last day of the New Year celebration. This is the first full moon of the new lunar year. It's a day when people explode fireworks in the streets, paint their faces, and dress up as . . .

B PAIR WORK Read your partner's entry. What do you like about it? Can you suggest anything to improve it?

8 CONVERSATION *Wedding day*

A ▶ Listen and practice.

Jill: Your wedding pictures are really beautiful, Emiko.

Emiko: Thank you. Those pictures are from right after the ceremony.

Jill: Where was the ceremony?

Emiko: At a shrine. When people get married in Japan, they sometimes have the ceremony at a shrine.

Jill: That's interesting. Were there a lot of people there?

Emiko: Well, usually only family members and close friends go to the ceremony. But afterward, we had a reception with family and friends.

Jill: So, what are receptions like in Japan?

Emiko: There's a big dinner, and after the meal, the guests give speeches or sing songs.

Jill: It sounds like fun.

Emiko: It really is. And then, before the guests leave, the bride and groom give them presents.

Jill: The guests get presents?

Emiko: Yes, and the guests give money to the bride and groom.

B ▶ Listen to the rest of the conversation. What did the bride and groom give each guest?

9 PRONUNCIATION *Stress and rhythm*

A ▶ Listen and practice. Notice how stressed words and syllables occur with a regular rhythm.

●　　　　●　　　　●　　　●　　　　　　●　　　　　●

When people get married in Japan, they sometimes have the ceremony at a shrine.

B ▶ Listen to the stress and rhythm in these sentences. Then practice them.

1. After the ceremony, there's a reception with family and friends.

2. Before the guests leave, the bride and groom give them presents.

3. The guests usually give money to the bride and groom.

10 GRAMMAR FOCUS

Adverbial clauses of time ▶

When people get married in Japan,	they sometimes have the ceremony at a shrine.
After the food is served,	the guests give speeches or sing songs.
Before the guests leave,	the bride and groom give them presents.

A What do you know about wedding customs in North America?
Complete these sentences with the information below.

1. Before a man and woman get married, they usually ....
2. When a couple gets engaged, the man often ....
3. Right after a couple gets engaged, they usually ....
4. When a woman gets married, her family usually ....
5. When guests go to a wedding, they almost always ....
6. Right after a couple gets married, they usually ....

a. pays for the wedding and reception.
b. go on a short trip called a "honeymoon."
c. give the bride and groom a gift or some money.
d. gives the woman an engagement ring.
e. begin to plan the wedding.
f. date each other for a year or more.

B PAIR WORK What happens when people get married in your country?
Tell your partner by completing the statements in part A with your own
information. Pay attention to stress and rhythm.

11 INTERCHANGE 8 Special occasions

How do your classmates celebrate special occasions? Go to Interchange 8 on page 122.

12 SPEAKING That's an interesting custom.

A GROUP WORK Do you know any interesting customs related to the
topics below? Explain a custom and discuss it with your classmates.

births   courtship   good luck   marriages   seasons

A: I know a custom from the Philippines. When a
boy courts a girl, he stands outside her house
and sings to her.
B: What does he sing?
C: Romantic songs, of course!

B CLASS ACTIVITY Tell the class the most interesting
custom you talked about in your group.

Customs Around the World

Look at the photos. What do you think is happening in each picture?

1 On the third Monday of October, Jamaicans celebrate National Heroes' Day. They honor seven men and women who were important to Jamaica's history. There are speeches, music, sports, and dancing. They also give awards to "local heroes" for helping their communities.

2 On August 15 of the lunar calendar, Koreans celebrate Chusok, also known as Korean Thanksgiving. It's a day when people give thanks for the harvest. Korean families honor their ancestors by going to their graves to take them rice and fruit and clean the gravesites.

3 An interesting custom in Thailand is Loy Krathong. A krathong is a bowl made from the bark and leaves of banana trees. It's decorated with a lit candle, three lit joss sticks, and flowers. After the rainy season, on the evening of the full moon in November, Thai people float krathongs on the river to pay respect to the river goddess.

4 Finland has a unique but very modern custom. It started because some people felt angry when their cell phones didn't work well. They wanted to express their frustration in a humorous way. So every summer, there is a cell-phone-throwing contest. People throw their cell phones as far as possible. The winner receives a prize, such as a gold medal.

A Read the article. Then answer these questions.

1. When is National Heroes' Day in Jamaica?
2. Why do Koreans celebrate Chusok?
3. What do Thais do for Loy Krathong?
4. Why do Finns go to the cell-phone-throwing contest?

B What do these words refer to? Write the correct word(s).

1. They (par. 1, line 2) ....
2. their (par. 1, line 6) ....
3. It (par. 2, line 3) ....

4. It (par. 3, line 3) ....
5. It (par. 4, line 2) ....
6. They (par. 4, line 4) ....

C **PAIR WORK** Do you have a similar holiday or custom in your country? Describe it.

Units 7–8 Progress check

SELF-ASSESSMENT

How well can you do these things? Check (✓) the boxes.

I can	Very well	OK	A little
Describe uses and purposes of everyday objects (Ex. 1)	☐	☐	☐
Give instructions and advice (Ex. 2)	☐	☐	☐
Describe special days and customs (Ex. 3, 5)	☐	☐	☐
Understand descriptions of customs (Ex. 4, 5)	☐	☐	☐
Ask and answer questions about special days and customs (Ex. 5)	☐	☐	☐

 GAME *What is it?*

A PAIR WORK Think of five familiar objects. Write a short description of each object's use and purpose. Don't write the name of the objects.

> It's electronic. You hold it in your hand. You look through it. You use it to make movies. It can sometimes be heavy.

B GROUP WORK Take turns reading your descriptions and guessing the objects. Keep score. Who guessed the most items correctly? Who wrote the best descriptions?

 ROLE PLAY *Stressful situations*

Student A: Choose one situation below. Decide on the details and answer Student B's questions. Then get some suggestions.
Start like this: *I'm really nervous. I'm* . . .

going on a job interview	**taking my driving test**	**giving a speech**
What's the job?	When is it?	What is it about?
What are the responsibilities?	How long is it?	Where is it?
Who is interviewing you?	Have you prepared?	How many people will be there?

Student B: Student A is telling you about a situation. Ask the appropriate questions above. Then give some suggestions.

Change roles and try the role play again.

useful expressions	
Try to . . .	Try not to . . .
Remember to . . .	Be sure to . . .
Don't forget to . . .	Make sure to . . .

3 SPEAKING *My own holiday*

A **PAIR WORK** Choose one of these imaginary holidays or create your own.
Then write a description of the holiday. Answer the questions below.

World Smile Day

All-You-Can-Eat Cake Day

Be Late for Something Day

What is the name of the holiday? When is it? How do you celebrate it?

> World Smile Day is a day when you have to smile at everyone. It's on June 15,
> the last day of school. People have parties, and sometimes there's a parade!

B **GROUP WORK** Read your description to the group. Then vote on the best holiday.

4 LISTENING *Marriage customs*

A ▶ Listen to some information about marriage customs. Check (✓) True or False.

True	False	
☐	☐	**1.** When two women of a tribe in Paraguay want to marry the same man, they have a boxing match. ....
☐	☐	**2.** When people get married in Malaysia, they have to eat cooked rice. ....
☐	☐	**3.** In Italy, before a couple gets married, a friend or relative releases two white doves. ....
☐	☐	**4.** In some parts of India, when people get married, water is poured over them. ....

B ▶ Listen again. Correct the false statements.

5 DISCUSSION *In my country, . . .*

GROUP WORK Talk about marriage in your country. Ask these questions and others of your own.

How old are people when they get married?
What happens after a couple gets engaged?
What happens during the ceremony?
What do the bride and groom wear?
What kind of food is served at the reception?
What kinds of gifts do people usually give?

a Korean wedding tradition

WHAT'S NEXT?

Look at your Self-assessment again. Do you need to review anything?

Times have changed!

1 SNAPSHOT

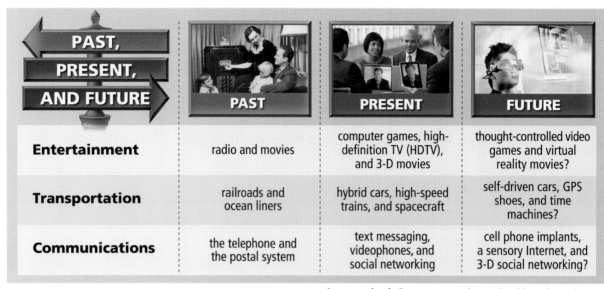

PAST, PRESENT, AND FUTURE	PAST	PRESENT	FUTURE
Entertainment	radio and movies	computer games, high-definition TV (HDTV), and 3-D movies	thought-controlled video games and virtual reality movies?
Transportation	railroads and ocean liners	hybrid cars, high-speed trains, and spacecraft	self-driven cars, GPS shoes, and time machines?
Communications	the telephone and the postal system	text messaging, videophones, and social networking	cell phone implants, a sensory Internet, and 3-D social networking?

Sources: www.futureforall.org; www.inventors.about.com; http://toptrends.nowandnext.com

Which of these past and present developments are the most important? Why?
Do you think any of the future developments could happen in your lifetime?
Can you think of two other developments that could happen in the future?

2 CONVERSATION *That's progress!*

A ⊙ Listen and practice.

Tanya: This neighborhood sure has changed!
 Matt: I know. A few years ago, not many people lived here. But the population is growing so fast these days.
Tanya: Remember how we used to rent videotapes at that little video store?
 Matt: Yeah. Now it's a multiplex cinema.
Tanya: And I hear they're tearing down our high school. They're going to build a shopping mall. Soon, there will be just malls and parking lots.
 Matt: That's because everyone has a car! Fifty years ago, people walked everywhere. Nowadays, they drive.
Tanya: That's progress, I guess.

B ⊙ Listen to the rest of the conversation.
What else has changed in their neighborhood?

GRAMMAR FOCUS

> ### Time contrasts ▶
>
> **Past**
> A few years ago, not many people **lived** here.
> People **used to rent** videotapes.
> Fifty years ago, people **walked** everywhere.
>
> **Present**
> These days, the population **is growing** so fast.
> Today, people **download** movies online.
> Nowadays, people **drive** their cars instead.
>
> **Future**
> Soon, there **will be** apartment blocks everywhere.
> In a few years, movie theaters **might not exist**.
> People **are going to have** self-driven cars in the future.

A Complete the sentences in column A with the appropriate information from column B. Then compare with a partner.

A

1. About 60 years ago, ...h.....
2. Before the automobile, ...
3. Before there were supermarkets, ...
4. In most offices these days, ...
5. In many cities nowadays, ...
6. In many classrooms today, ...
7. In the next 100 years, ...
8. Sometime in the near future, ...

B

a. people used to shop at small grocery stores.
b. pollution is becoming a serious problem.
c. students are learning with interactive whiteboards.
d. people didn't travel as much from city to city.
e. there will probably be cities in space.
f. people work more than 40 hours a week.
g. doctors might find a cure for the common cold.
h. many TV shows were in black and white.

B Complete four of the phrases in part A, column A, with your own ideas. Then compare with a partner.

4

PRONUNCIATION   Intonation in statements with time phrases

A ▶ Listen and practice. Notice the intonation in these statements beginning with a time phrase.

In the past, very few people used computers.

Today, people use computers all the time.

In the future, there will be a computer in every home.

B **PAIR WORK** Complete these statements with your own information. Then read your statements to a partner. Pay attention to intonation.

As a child, I used to . . .   These days, . . .
Five years ago, I . . .   In five years, I'll . . .
Nowadays, I . . .   In ten years, I might . . .

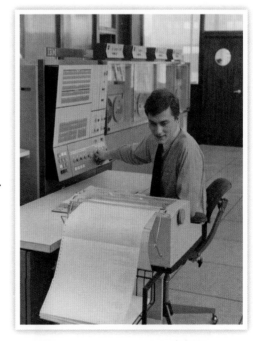

5 LISTENING *For better or for worse*

A ⏵ Listen to people discuss changes. Check (✓) the topic each person talks about.

Topic			Change	Better or worse?	
1. ☐ population	☐ environment	....		☐	☐
2. ☐ transportation	☐ cities	....		☐	☐
3. ☐ families	☐ shopping	....		☐	☐

B ⏵ Listen again. Write down the change and check (✓) if things are better or worse now.

6 SPEAKING *Changing times*

GROUP WORK How have things changed? How will things be different in the future? Choose four of these topics. Then discuss the questions below.

education	fashion	shopping
entertainment	food	sports
environment	housing	technology

What was it like in the past?
What is it like today?
What will it be like in the future?

A: In the past, people listened to sports on the radio.
B: Nowadays, they can watch sports on HDTVs , too.
C: In the future, . . .

7 WRITING *A description of a person*

A **PAIR WORK** Interview your partner about his or her past, present, and hopes for the future.

B Write a paragraph describing how your partner has changed. Make some predictions about the future. Don't write your partner's name.

> This person moved to our school several years ago.
> She used to be the quietest girl in the class. Now,
> she's in the drama club and loves to watch soap operas.
> Someday, she'll be a successful actress. She'll be famous.
> She'll star in movies and on TV. I think she'll . . .

C **CLASS ACTIVITY** Read your paragraph to the class. Can they guess who it is about?

8 PERSPECTIVES *Take the good with the bad.*

A ▶ Listen to some possible consequences of getting a high-paying job. Check (✓) the statements you agree with.

If you get a high-paying job, . . .

.... you'll have more cash to spend.
.... you'll be able to buy anything you want.
.... you'll be able to travel first class.
.... you might have to pay higher taxes.
.... you'll be able to donate more to charities.
.... more people may want to be your friend.
.... you may get your own office.
.... you won't have as much stress in your life.
.... people will ask you for a loan.
.... you'll have a lot more free time.

B **PAIR WORK** Look at the statements again. Which are advantages of getting a high-paying job? Which are disadvantages?

"The first one is an advantage. Everyone would like to have more money!"

9 GRAMMAR FOCUS

Conditional sentences with if clauses ▶

Possible situation (present)	Consequence (future with will, may, or might)
If you **get** a high-paying job,	you**'ll have** more cash to spend.
If you **have** more cash to spend,	you**'ll be able to buy** anything you want.
If you **can buy** anything you want,	you **won't save** your money.
If you **don't save** your money,	you **may need** another job.

A Match the *if* clauses in column A with the appropriate consequences from column B. Then compare with a partner.

A

1. If you eat less sugar, ...
2. If you walk to work every day, ...
3. If you don't get enough sleep, ...
4. If you change jobs, ...
5. If you don't get married, ...
6. If you travel abroad, ...

B

a. you'll be able to experience a new culture.
b. you might feel a lot healthier.
c. you'll stay in shape without joining a gym.
d. you'll have more money to spend on yourself.
e. you won't be able to stay awake in class.
f. you may not like it better than your old one.

B Add your own consequences to the *if* clauses in column A. Then practice with a partner.

"If you eat less sugar, you'll lose weight."

10 WORD POWER Consequences

A **PAIR WORK** Can you find two consequences for each possible situation?
Complete the chart with information from the list.

communicate in a different language
earn your own spending money
experience culture shock
feel jealous sometimes
get in shape
get into a good college
get married
get valuable work experience
improve your grades
pay membership dues

Possible situation	Consequences
fall in love	....
get a part-time job	....
join a gym	....
move to a foreign country	....
study very hard	....

B **GROUP WORK** Share your answers with the group. Can you think of
one more consequence for each event?

11 SPEAKING Unexpected consequences

A **GROUP WORK** Choose three possible events from Exercise 10.
One student completes an event with a consequence. The next
student adds a consequence. Suggest at least five consequences.

A: If you study very hard, you'll improve your grades.
B: If you improve your grades, you'll get into a good school.
C: If you get into a good school, you may get a good job.
D: If you get a good job, you'll make a lot of money.
A: If you make a lot of money, you may have more stress.

B **CLASS ACTIVITY** Who has the most interesting consequences for each event?

12 INTERCHANGE 9 Consider the consequences

Give your opinion about some issues. Go to Interchange 9 on page 123.

❧ Are you in LOVE? ❧

What is the difference between "having a crush" on someone and falling in love?

You think you're falling in love. You're really attracted to a certain person. But this has happened before, and it was just a "crush." How can you tell if it's real this time? Here's what our readers said:

If you're falling in love, . . .

♥ you'll find yourself talking to, calling, or texting the person for no reason. (You might pretend there's a reason, but often there's not.)

♥ you'll find yourself bringing this person into every conversation. ("When I was in Mexico – ," a friend begins. You interrupt with, "My boyfriend made a great Mexican dinner last week.")

♥ you might suddenly be interested in things you used to avoid. ("When a woman asks me to tell her all about football, I know she's fallen in love," said a TV sports announcer.)

OK, so you've fallen in love. But falling in love is one thing, and staying in love is another. How can you tell, as time passes, that you're still in love?

If you stay in love, your relationship will change. You might not talk as much about the person you are in love with. You might not call him or her so often. But this person will nevertheless become more and more important in your life.

You'll find that you can be yourself with this person. When you first fell in love, you were probably afraid to admit certain things about yourself. But now you can be totally honest. You can trust him or her to accept you just as you are. Falling in love is great – staying in love is even better!

A Read the article. Where do you think it is from? Check (✓) the correct answer.

☐ an online news service ☐ a magazine ☐ an advice column ☐ an advertisement

B What things happen when you're falling in love compared with staying in love? Complete the chart.

Falling in love	Staying in love
1.	1. ....
2.	2. ....
3.	3. ....

C **PAIR WORK** Which do you think is more difficult – falling in love or staying in love? Can you think of other signs of being in love?

10 I hate working on weekends.

1 SNAPSHOT

EIGHT IMPORTANT JOB SKILLS

Here are some questions that employers might ask about your skills.

- ☐ 1. Can you **use a computer**?
- ☐ 2. Can you **manage other people**?
- ☐ 3. Are you **good at public speaking**?
- ☐ 4. Can you **teach others** how to do things?

- ☐ 5. Can you **solve problems**?
- ☐ 6. Do you **manage money well**?
- ☐ 7. Do you **work well with people**?
- ☐ 8. Do you **speak other languages**?

Source: U.S. Department of Labor

Which of these skills do you think are most important? Why?
Check (✔) the skills that you think you have.
Look at the skills you checked. What jobs do you think you might be good at?

2 CONVERSATION *I need a job!*

A ▶ Listen and practice.

Dan: I'm so broke. I really need to find a job!

Brad: So do I. Do you see anything good listed?

Dan: How about this telephone sales job? You call people and try to sell them magazines.

Brad: That sounds boring. And anyway, I'm not very good at selling.

Dan: Well, I am! I might check that one out. Oh, here's one for you. An assistant entertainment director on a cruise ship.

Brad: That sounds like fun. I love traveling, and I've never been on a cruise ship.

Dan: It says here you have to work every day while the ship is at sea.

Brad: That's OK. I don't mind working long hours if the pay is good. I think I'll apply for it.

B ▶ Listen to Brad's phone call. What else does the job require?

GRAMMAR FOCUS

> ### Gerunds; short responses ▸

Affirmative statements with gerunds	Agree	Disagree	Other verbs or phrases followed by gerunds
I love traveling.	So do I.	I don't.	
I hate working on weekends.	So do I.	Really? I like it.	
I'm good at using a computer.	So am I.	Oh, I'm not.	like
Negative statements with gerunds			enjoy
I don't mind working long hours.	Neither do I.	I do.	be interested in
I'm not good at selling.	Neither am I.	Well, I am.	
I can't stand commuting.	Neither can I.	Oh, I don't mind.	

A PAIR WORK Match the phrases in columns A and B to make statements about yourself. Then take turns reading your sentences and giving short responses.

A
1. I hate ....
2. I'm not very good at ....
3. I'm good at ....
4. I don't like ....
5. I can't stand ....
6. I'm interested in ....
7. I don't mind ....
8. I enjoy ....

B
a. talking on the phone.
b. working with a group or team.
c. solving other people's problems.
d. sitting in long meetings.
e. working on weekends.
f. eating lunch out every day.
g. managing my time.
h. learning foreign languages.

A: I hate working on weekends.
B: So do I.

B GROUP WORK Complete the phrases in column A with your own information. Then take turns reading your statements. Ask questions to get more information.

4 **PRONUNCIATION** *Unreleased and released* /t/ *and* /d/

A ▸ Listen and practice. Notice that when the sound /t/ or /d/ at the end of a word is followed by a consonant, it's unreleased. When it is followed by a vowel sound, it's released.

Unreleased
She's not good at math and science.

I hate working on Sundays.

You need to manage money well.

Released
He's not a good artist.

They really hate it!

I need a cup of coffee.

B PAIR WORK Write three sentences starting with *I'm not very good at* and *I don't mind*. Then practice the sentences. Pay attention to the unreleased and released sounds /t/ and /d/.

SPEAKING *The right job*

A **PAIR WORK** How does your partner feel about doing these things?
Interview your partner. Check (✓) his or her answers.

How do you feel about . . . ?	I enjoy it.	I don't mind it.	I hate it.
asking for help	☐	☐	☐
using a computer	☐	☐	☐
leading a team	☐	☐	☐
traveling	☐	☐	☐
creating spreadsheets	☐	☐	☐
talking on the phone	☐	☐	☐
working with people	☐	☐	☐
meeting deadlines	☐	☐	☐
working on the weekend	☐	☐	☐
managing money	☐	☐	☐
telling people what to do	☐	☐	☐
working with numbers	☐	☐	☐
public speaking	☐	☐	☐

B **PAIR WORK** Look back at the information in part A. Suggest a job for your partner.

"You enjoy creating spreadsheets and working with numbers. And you don't mind
managing money. I think you'd be a good accountant."

6 **LISTENING** *Job hunting*

A ▶ Listen to people talk about the kind of work they are looking for.
Check (✓) the job that would be best for each person.

1. Bill
   ☐ flight attendant
   ☐ teacher
   ☐ songwriter

2. Shannon
   ☐ lawyer
   ☐ bookkeeper
   ☐ doctor

3. Ben
   ☐ marine biologist
   ☐ model
   ☐ architect

B ▶ Listen again. Answer these questions.

1. What kind of job is Bill *not* interested in? ....
2. What is his attitude toward making money? ....
3. What do Shannon's family members do for a living? ....
4. What does she want to do before she gets a job? ....
5. What has Ben done to break into movies? ....
6. What does he show the interviewer? ....

7 **INTERCHANGE 10** *Dream job*

Decide which job to apply for. Go to Interchange 10 on page 124.

8 WORD POWER Personality traits

A Which of these adjectives are positive (**P**)? Which are negative (**N**)?

creative	....P....	impatient	....
critical	....	level-headed	....
disorganized	....	moody	....
efficient	....	punctual	....
forgetful	....	reliable	....
generous	....	short-tempered	....
hardworking	....	strict	....

creative

B PAIR WORK Tell your partner about people you know with these personality traits.

"My neighbor is short-tempered. Sometimes he . . ."

C ▶ Listen to four conversations. Then check (✓) the adjective that best describes each person.

impatient

1. a boss
   - ☐ creative
   - ☐ forgetful
   - ☐ serious

2. a co-worker
   - ☐ unfriendly
   - ☐ generous
   - ☐ strange

3. a teacher
   - ☐ moody
   - ☐ patient
   - ☐ hardworking

4. a relative
   - ☐ short-tempered
   - ☐ disorganized
   - ☐ reliable

9 PERSPECTIVES Job profiles

A ▶ Listen to these people answer the question, "What kind of work would you like to do?" What job does each person talk about?

"Well, I think I'd make a good journalist because I'm good at writing. When I was in college, I worked as a reporter for the school website. I really enjoyed writing different kinds of articles."

"I know what I *don't* want to do! A lot of my friends work in the stock market, but I could never be a stockbroker because I can't make decisions quickly. I don't mind working hard, but I'm terrible under pressure!"

"I'm still in school. My parents want me to be a teacher, but I'm not sure yet. I guess I could be a teacher because I'm very creative. I'm also very impatient, so maybe I shouldn't work with kids."

B PAIR WORK Look at the interviews again. Who are you most like? least like? Why?

10 GRAMMAR FOCUS

Clauses with because

The word **because** *introduces a cause or reason.*

I'd make a good journalist **because I'm good at writing**.
I could be a teacher **because I'm very creative**.
I wouldn't want to be a teacher **because I'm very impatient**.
I could never be a stockbroker **because I can't make decisions quickly**.

A Complete the sentences in column A with appropriate information from column B. Then compare with a partner.

A

1. I wouldn't want to be a nurse ....
2. I'd like to be a novelist ....
3. I could never be an accountant ....
4. I would make a bad waiter ....
5. I could be a flight attendant ....
6. I'd never work on a cruise ship ....

B

a. because I don't like hospitals.
b. because I really enjoy traveling.
c. because I have a terrible memory.
d. because I get seasick very easily.
e. because I love creative writing.
f. because I'm terrible with numbers.

B GROUP WORK Think about your personal qualities and skills. Then complete these statements. Take turns discussing them with your group.

I could never be a . . . because . . .
I wouldn't mind working as a . . . because . . .

I'd make a good . . . because . . .
The best job for me is . . . because . . .

11 WRITING *A cover letter for a job application*

A Imagine you are applying for one of the jobs in this unit. Write a short cover letter for a job application.

Mr. Yoshioka
Personnel Director
Executive Airlines

Dear Mr. Yoshioka,
    I am responding to your recent advertisement in *The Post* for a bilingual international flight attendant. I think I'd make a good flight attendant for Executive Air Lines because I'm a very friendly person and I really love traveling. I also enjoy meeting people.
    As you can see from my résumé, I've had a lot of experience working with tourists. I worked at . . .

B PAIR WORK Exchange papers. If you received this letter, would you invite the applicant for a job interview? Why or why not?

Find the Job That's Right for You!

Look at the photo and skim the list of personality types. Which one best describes the person in the picture?

1 About half of all workers in the United States have jobs they aren't happy with. Don't let this happen to you! If you want to find the right job, don't rush to look through job ads on the Internet. Instead, sit down and think about yourself. What kind of person are you? What makes you happy?

2 According to psychologist John Holland, there are six types of personalities. Nobody is just one personality type, but most people are mainly one type. For each type, there are certain jobs that might be right and others that are probably wrong.

3 Considering your personality type can help you make the right job decision. Liz is a good example. Liz knew she wanted to do something for children. She thought she could help children as a school counselor or a lawyer. She took counseling and law courses – and hated them. After talking to a career counselor, she realized that she's an Artistic type. Liz studied film, and she now produces children's TV shows – and loves it.

Personality types

The Realistic type
is practical and likes working with machines and tools.

The Investigative type
is curious and likes to learn, analyze situations, and solve problems.

The Artistic type
is imaginative and likes to express ideas by creating art.

The Social type
is friendly and likes helping or training other people.

The Enterprising type
is outgoing and likes to persuade or lead other people.

The Conventional type
is careful and likes to follow routines and keep track of details.

A Read the article. Then find these sentences in the article. Is each sentence the main idea or a supporting idea in that paragraph? Check (✓) the correct boxes.

	Main idea	Supporting idea
1. About half of all workers . . . they aren't happy with. (par. 1)	☐	☐
2. According to psychologist . . . types of personalities. (par. 2)	☐	☐
3. For each type, there are . . . that are probably wrong. (par. 2)	☐	☐
4. Considering your personality . . . the right job decision. (par. 3)	☐	☐
5. After talking to a career counselor, . . . an Artistic type. (par. 3)	☐	☐

B For each personality type, write two examples of appropriate jobs. Then explain your answers to a partner.

Realistic	Investigative	Artistic	Social	Enterprising	Conventional
....	....	....	....	....	....
....	....	....	....	....	....

C **GROUP WORK** What personality type do you think you are? Does your group agree?

Units 9–10 Progress check

SELF-ASSESSMENT

How well can you do these things? Check (✓) the boxes.

I can	Very well	OK	A little
Describe people and things in the past, present, and future (Ex. 1)	☐	☐	☐
Describe possible consequences of actions (Ex. 2)	☐	☐	☐
Understand descriptions of abilities and personalities (Ex. 3, 4)	☐	☐	☐
Ask and answer questions about preferences and skills (Ex. 4)	☐	☐	☐
Give reasons for my opinions (Ex. 4)	☐	☐	☐

1 SPEAKING *Past, present, and future*

A **PAIR WORK** Think of one more question for each category. Then interview a partner.

Appearance   What did you use to look like? Can you describe yourself now?
                 What do you think you'll look like in the future?

Free time   Did you have a hobby as a child? What do you like to do these days?
                 How are you going to spend your free time next year?

B **GROUP WORK** Share one interesting thing about your partner.

2 GAME *Truth and consequences*

A Add two situations and two consequences to the lists below.

Situation	Consequence
☐ you move to a foreign country	☐ buy you a gift
☐ it's sunny tomorrow	☐ feel jealous sometimes
☐ it's cold tomorrow	☐ communicate in a new language
☐ you give me $10	☐ go to the beach
☐ you don't call me later	☐ get really angry
☐ you fall in love	☐ stay home
☐	☐ ....
☐	☐ ....

B **CLASS ACTIVITY** Go around the class and make sentences. Check (✓) each *if* clause after you use it. The student who uses the most clauses correctly wins.

"If you move to a foreign country, you'll learn to . . ."

3 LISTENING *Good or bad?*

A ● Listen to Louisa and Tim discuss four jobs. Write down the jobs and check (✓) if they would be good or bad at them.

	Job	Good	Bad	Reason
1. Louisa	....	☐	☐	....
	....	☐	☐	....
2. Tim	....	☐	☐	....
	....	☐	☐	....

B ● Listen again. What reasons do they give?

4 DISCUSSION *Job profile*

A Prepare a personal job profile. Write your name, skills, and job preferences. Think about the questions below. Then compare with a partner.

Are you good at . . . ?
communicating with people
solving problems
making decisions quickly
speaking foreign languages

Do you . . . ?
have any special skills
have any experience
have a good memory
manage money well

Do you mind . . . ?
traveling
working with a team
wearing a uniform
working long hours

A: Are you good at communicating with people?
B: Sure. I enjoy talking to people.
A: So do I. I like meeting new people and . . .

B GROUP WORK Make suggestions for possible jobs based on your classmates' job profiles. Give reasons for your opinions. What do you think of their suggestions for you?

A: Juan would be a good executive because he likes solving problems and making decisions quickly.
B: No way! I could never be an executive. I'm too disorganized!

WHAT'S NEXT?

Look at your Self-assessment again. Do you need to review anything?

11 It's really worth seeing!

SNAPSHOT

MODERN **Wonders**

| The Lotus Temple in Delhi, India, was finished in 1986. Its lotus-shaped leaves are made of marble. | The Museum of Contemporary Art in Niterói, Brazil, is a modern, saucer-shaped structure. | The Millau Viaduct, over the Tam River in France, was opened in 2004. It's the tallest bridge in the world. | The National Stadium in Beijing, China, is also known as the Bird's Nest because of its unique appearance. | The Palm Islands of Dubai, U.A.E., were designed to look like palm trees. Construction was started in 2001. |

Sources: http://science.discovery.com; www.thinkquest.org

Which of these wonders do you think is the most amazing? Why?
What other modern wonders do you know about? What are they? Where are they?
What modern wonders are in your country?

2 PERSPECTIVES *The Empire State Building*

A How much do you know about the Empire State Building?
Check (✓) the statements you think are true.

- ☐ 1. It was designed by an American architect.
- ☐ 2. It is in New York City.
- ☐ 3. It was officially opened by the president of the United States in 1931.
- ☐ 4. It took five years to build.
- ☐ 5. It cost $2 million to build.
- ☐ 6. There are 102 floors in the building.
- ☐ 7. There are colored lights at the top.
- ☐ 8. It is the tallest building in the world.

B ▶ Now listen and check your answers. What information is the most surprising?

Passive with by (simple past) ▶

The passive changes the focus of a sentence.
For the simple past, use the past of **be** *+ past participle.*

Active
The president **opened** the building in 1931.
An American architect **designed** the building.
In 1964, the building's owners **added**
    colored lights to the top.

Passive
It **was opened by** the president in 1931.
It **was designed by** an American architect.
Colored lights **were added** to the top **by**
    the building's owners in 1964.

A Complete the sentences with the simple past passive
form of the verbs. Then compare with a partner.

1. The 2010 World Cup final .... (win) by Spain.
2. The film *Avatar* .... (direct) by James Cameron.
3. The novel *The Adventures of Huckleberry Finn*
   .... (write) by Mark Twain.
4. The songs "Revolution" and "Hey Jude" ....
   (record) by the Beatles in 1968.
5. *The Starry Night* .... (paint) by
   Vincent van Gogh.
6. The Shanghai Grand Theater .... (design)
   by French architect Jean-Marie Charpentier.
7. The opening ceremony of the 2012 London Olympics
   .... (see) by billions of people.
8. In the 2007 film *I'm Not There*, the American musician
   Bob Dylan .... (play) by six different
   people, including Australian actress Cate Blanchett.

B **PAIR WORK** Change these sentences into passive sentences with *by*.
Then take turns reading them aloud.

1. Sculptor Frédéric-Auguste Bartholdi designed the Statue of Liberty in 1884.
   ....

2. Daniel Day-Lewis played Abraham Lincoln in the 2012 film *Lincoln*.
   ....

3. Gabriel García Márquez wrote the book *One Hundred Years of Solitude* in 1971.
   ....

4. Woo Paik produced the first digital HDTV in 1991.
   ....

5. J. K. Rowling wrote the first Harry Potter book on an old manual typewriter.
   ....

6. *Empire* magazine readers chose *The Godfather* as the greatest film of all time.
   ....

4 **INTERCHANGE 11** *Who is this by?*

Who created these well-known works? Go to Interchange 11 on page 125.

5 PRONUNCIATION *The letter o*

A ⊙ Listen and practice. Notice how the letter *o* is pronounced in the following words.

/a/	/ou/	/uː/	/ʌ/
not	no	do	one
top	don't	food	love
....	....	....	....
....	....	....	....

B ⊙ How is the letter *o* pronounced in these words? Write them in the correct column in part A. Then listen and check your answers.

come   done   lock   own   shot   soon   who   wrote

6 LISTENING *Who built them?*

⊙ Listen to three tour guides describe some very old monuments.
Take notes to answer the questions below. Then compare with a partner.

the pyramids

Who built them?
Why were they built?

Machu Picchu

How big is the city?
When was it discovered?

the Great Wall of China

Why was it built?
How long is it?

7 WORD POWER *Local industry*

A Complete the chart. Then add one more word to each category.

cattle   oysters
✓ corn   sheep
electronics   shrimp
goats   soybeans
✓ lobsters   textiles
microchips   wheat

Farmed	Grown	Manufactured	Raised
lobsters	corn	....	....
....	....	....	....
....	....	....	....
....	....	....	....

B GROUP WORK Talk about things that are found in your country.

"We grow soybeans. We also manufacture cars."

8 CONVERSATION *I need some information.*

A ▶ Listen and practice.

Kelly: Hello?
John: Oh, hello. I need some information. What currency is used in the European Union?
Kelly: Where?
John: The European Union.
Kelly: I think the euro is used in most of Europe.
John: Oh, right. And is English spoken much there?
Kelly: I really have no idea.
John: Huh? Well, what about credit cards? Are they accepted everywhere?
Kelly: How would I know?
John: Well, you're a travel agent, aren't you?
Kelly: What? This is a hair salon. You have the wrong number!

B PAIR WORK Use information about a country you know to act out the conversation.

9 GRAMMAR FOCUS

Passive without by (simple present) ▶

For the simple present, use the present of be + past participle.

Active	Passive
They **use** the euro in most of Europe.	The euro **is used** in most of Europe.
They **speak** English in many European countries.	English **is spoken** in many European countries.
They **manufacture** a lot of cars in Europe.	A lot of cars **are manufactured** in Europe.

A Complete this passage using the simple present passive form.

Many crops .... (grow) in Taiwan. Some crops .... (consume) locally, but others .... (export). Tea .... (grow) in cooler parts of the island, and rice .... (cultivate) in warmer parts. Fishing is also an important industry. A wide variety of seafood .... (catch) and .... (ship) all over the world. Many people .... (employ) in the electronics and textile industries as well.

B Complete the sentences. Use the passive of these verbs.

grow   make up   manufacture   raise   speak   use

1. French and English .... in Canada.
2. A lot of rice .... in Vietnam.
3. The U.S. .... of 50 states.
4. A lot of sheep .... in New Zealand.
5. Cars and computers .... in Korea.
6. The U.S. dollar .... in Ecuador.

C PAIR WORK Use the passive of the verbs in part B to talk about your country and other countries you know.

10 LISTENING Colombia

A ▶ Listen to a short talk about Colombia. Complete the chart.

Facts about Colombia	
Location	....
Population	....
Language	....
Industries	....
Agricultural products	....

Bogotá, Colombia

B ▶ Listen again. Check (✓) the things the speaker mentions about Colombia.

☐ beaches   ☐ volcanoes   ☐ snow-capped mountains
☐ rivers   ☐ lakes   ☐ hot lowland plains

11 SPEAKING Guess the country

A PAIR WORK Choose a country. Then answer these questions.

Where is it located?   What currency is used?
What cities are found there?   What famous tourist attraction is found there?
What languages are spoken?   What products are exported?

B CLASS ACTIVITY Give a short talk like the one in Exercise 10 about the country you chose. Don't say the country's name. Can the class guess the country?

12 WRITING A guidebook introduction

A Make an information chart like the one in Exercise 10 about a country you know. Then write an introduction for a guidebook about the country.

> Vietnam is located in Southeast Asia. It has a population of over 90 million people. Vietnamese is the official language. The country has many beautiful beaches, high mountains, and busy cities. Rice is grown in . . .

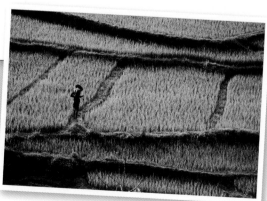

B GROUP WORK Exchange papers. Is any important information missing? Ask questions to find out more.

A Guide to *Unusual* Museums

Look at the pictures and scan the article. Where do you think you can see very old objects? a working factory? historic cooking tools?

1 Have you been to the Louvre in Paris, the National Museum of Anthropology in Mexico City, or any of those other "must see" museums? Well, now it's time to go off the beaten path.

The Kimchi Museum
Seoul, South Korea

The Museum of Gold
Bogotá, Colombia

The Chocolate Museum
Cologne, Germany

2 If you don't know about kimchi, a trip to the Kimchi Museum is an eye-opening experience. The museum was founded in 1986 to highlight South Korea's rich kimchi culture. The exhibit includes displays of cooking utensils and materials related to making, storing, and eating the famous pickled vegetables. The museum also provides details about the history and nutritional benefits of South Korea's most beloved side dish. Finally, stop by the souvenir shop to try various types of kimchi.

3 If you want to see beautiful objects, the Museum of Gold is the place. It holds one of South America's most stunning collections. Because the exhibits sparkle so brightly, you can actually take photographs without using a flash on your camera! Not everything is made of gold, though. Among the exhibits are ancient pre-Columbian items. Many of them are made from a mixture of gold and copper, known as tumbaga.

4 The Chocolate Museum will teach you everything about chocolate – from cocoa bean to candy bars. You'll learn about chocolate's 3,000-year history and discover how it was once used as money in South America. A real chocolate factory shows you how chocolate is made. After you've finished the tour, you can sample a complimentary drink of rich, gooey pure chocolate – perfect for those with a sweet tooth.

A Read the article. Find the words in *italics* below in the article. Then circle the meaning of each word or phrase.

1. When you *go off the beaten path*, you **do something unusual / go somewhere far away**.
2. When something is *founded*, it is **started / discovered**.
3. When something is *stunning*, it is extremely **attractive / large**.
4. When something is *ancient*, it is **very old / common**.
5. When something is *complimentary*, it is **free of charge / very expensive**.
6. When something is *gooey*, it is **light and refreshing / thick and sticky**.

B Where do these sentences belong? Write the number of the paragraph where each sentence could go.

.... a. Don't forget to buy your favorite kind to bring home for dinner!
.... b. Did you know that it wasn't popular in Europe until the nineteenth century?
.... c. The museum also features coins, jewelry, and pieces of rare art.
.... d. There are some museums that try to be a little different.

C **PAIR WORK** Which of these museums would you most like to visit? Why?

It's really worth seeing! ■ 77

12 What happened?

1 SNAPSHOT

Aha!

Where did the ideas for these "accidental inventions" come from?

The Popsicle

In 1905, 11-year-old Frank Epperson wanted to make a new soft drink. He mixed the ingredients with a stick, but he left the soda outside overnight. The next morning, he found it frozen with the stick inside.

Velcro

In 1948 George de Mestral went for a walk and noticed small seeds stuck to his clothes. He examined them under a microscope and found hundreds of small hooks that stuck to almost anything.

Post-it Notes

In 1970 Spencer Silver tried to invent a new glue, but it was very weak. No one wanted to use it. Four years later, his co-worker Arthur Fry put the glue on bookmarks to keep them in place.

Sources: http://inventors.about.com

Which of these accidental inventions do you think is the most interesting? the most useful?
Do you know of any other things that were invented accidentally?

2 PERSPECTIVES *It happened to me!*

A ▶ Listen to what happened to these people. Check (✓) the things that have happened to you.

☐ "I was watching a really good movie, but I fell asleep before the end."

☐ "I was traveling in another country when I met an old school friend."

☐ "While I was shopping one day, a celebrity walked into the store."

☐ "I was talking to my friend when my cell phone died."

☐ "I was getting off a bus when I slipped and fell on the sidewalk."

☐ "I was typing my book report on my computer when it crashed."

☐ "While I was walking down the street, I found some money."

B Choose one statement that you checked. What happened next?

"I recharged my cell phone and called my friend back."

Past continuous vs. simple past ▶

Use the past continuous for an action in progress in the past.
Use the simple past for an action that interrupts it.

I **was watching** a good movie,	but I **fell** asleep before the end.
I **was talking** to my friend	when my cell phone **died**.
While I **was shopping** one day,	a celebrity **walked** into the store.

A Complete these sentences. Then compare with a partner.

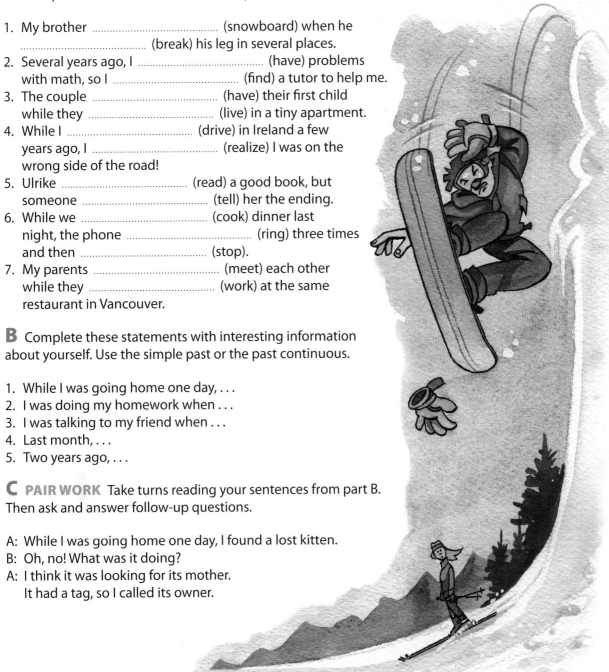

1. My brother .... (snowboard) when he
   .... (break) his leg in several places.
2. Several years ago, I .... (have) problems
   with math, so I .... (find) a tutor to help me.
3. The couple .... (have) their first child
   while they .... (live) in a tiny apartment.
4. While I .... (drive) in Ireland a few
   years ago, I .... (realize) I was on the
   wrong side of the road!
5. Ulrike .... (read) a good book, but
   someone .... (tell) her the ending.
6. While we .... (cook) dinner last
   night, the phone .... (ring) three times
   and then .... (stop).
7. My parents .... (meet) each other
   while they .... (work) at the same
   restaurant in Vancouver.

B Complete these statements with interesting information
about yourself. Use the simple past or the past continuous.

1. While I was going home one day, . . .
2. I was doing my homework when . . .
3. I was talking to my friend when . . .
4. Last month, . . .
5. Two years ago, . . .

C PAIR WORK Take turns reading your sentences from part B.
Then ask and answer follow-up questions.

A: While I was going home one day, I found a lost kitten.
B: Oh, no! What was it doing?
A: I think it was looking for its mother.
   It had a tag, so I called its owner.

4 LISTENING Lucky breaks

A ▶ Listen to these stories about lucky breaks. What were
the people doing before they got their lucky breaks? What were
their lucky breaks?

	What they were doing	Lucky break
1. Yang Zhifa	....	....
2. Gwyneth Paltrow	....	....

Terracotta warriors

B ▶ Listen again. How did the events change their lives?

5 WORD POWER Storytelling

A Some adverbs are often used in storytelling to emphasize that something
interesting is about to happen. Which of these adverbs are positive (**P**)?
Which are negative (**N**)? Which could be either (**E**)?

coincidentally	....	strangely	....
fortunately	....	suddenly	....
luckily	....	surprisingly	....
miraculously	....	unexpectedly	....
sadly	....	unfortunately	....

B **PAIR WORK** Complete these statements with
adverbs from part A to make up creative sentences.

I was walking down the street when, . . .
It started out as a normal day, but, . . .
We were on our way to the party when, . . .

A: I was walking down the street when, unexpectedly,
I saw a celebrity!
B: Or, I was walking down the street when, suddenly,
I looked down and found $20!

6 WRITING A recent event

A Write a short story about something that happened to you recently.
Try to include some of the adverbs from Exercise 5.

> I was visiting the coast last year when, unexpectedly, I got a chance to go
> kayaking. Fortunately, it was a perfect day, and I was having a great time. The
> water was calm, and I was beginning to feel a little tired when, suddenly, . . .

B **GROUP WORK** Take turns reading your stories. Answer any questions from the group.

CONVERSATION *What have you been doing?*

A ▶ Listen and practice.

Pete: Hey, Gina! I haven't seen you in ages.
        What have you been doing lately?
Gina: Nothing exciting. I've been working
        two jobs for the last six months.
Pete: How come?
Gina: I'm saving up money for a trip to Morocco.
Pete: Well, that's exciting.
Gina: Yeah, it is. What about you?
Pete: Well, I've only been *spending* money. I'm
        pursuing a full-time modeling career.
Gina: Really? How long have you been modeling?
Pete: Since I graduated. But I haven't been getting any
        work lately. I need a job soon. I'm almost out of money!

B ▶ Listen to two other people at the party. What has
happened since they last saw each other?

8 **GRAMMAR FOCUS**

> **Present perfect continuous** ▶
>
> *Use the present perfect continuous for actions that*
> *start in the past and continue into the present.*
> What **have** you **been doing** lately? I'**ve been working** two jobs for the last six months.
> How long **have** you **been modeling**? I'**ve been modeling** since I graduated.
> **Have** you **been saving** money? No, I **haven't been saving** money. I'**ve been spending** it!

A Complete the conversations with the present perfect continuous.

1. A: What .... you .... (do) lately?
   B: Well, I .... (spend) my free time at the beach.

2. A: .... you .... (work) part-time this year?
   B: Yes, I have. I .... (make) sandwiches at
      the Lunch Time Café for the past few months.

3. A: How .... you .... (feel) recently?
   B: Great! I .... (get) a lot of sleep. And I ....
      (not drink) as much coffee since I stopped working at the coffee shop.

4. A: .... you .... (get) enough exercise lately?
   B: No, I haven't. I .... (study) a lot for a big exam.

B **PAIR WORK** Read the conversations in part A together. Then read them again and answer the
questions with your own information.

A: What have you been doing lately?
B: I've been listening to a lot of classical music. It helps me study.

9 PRONUNCIATION *Contrastive stress in responses*

A ▶ Listen and practice. Notice how the stress changes to emphasize a contrast.

A: Has your brother been studying German?

B: No, I've been studying German.

A: Have you been teaching French?

B: No, I've been studying French.

B ▶ Mark the stress changes in these conversations. Listen and check. Then practice the conversations.

A: Have you been studying for ten years?

B: No, I've been studying for two years.

A: Have you been studying at school?

B: No, I've been studying at home.

10 SPEAKING *Tell me about it.*

GROUP WORK Add three questions to this list. Then take turns asking and answering the questions. Remember to ask for further information.

Have you been . . . lately?

taking any lessons
working out
learning a new hobby
working long hours
reading any good books
playing any cool video games
traveling
staying up late

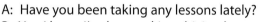

useful expressions

Really?
I didn't know that!
Oh, I see.
I had no idea.
Wow! Tell me more.

A: Have you been taking any lessons lately?
B: Yes, I have. I've been taking driving lessons.
C: Really? How's that going?
B: Great! I think I'm becoming an excellent driver.

11 INTERCHANGE 12 *Life is like a game!*

Play a board game. Go to Interchange 12 on page 126.

From the Streets to the Screen

Skim the article. What makes Staff Benda Bilili different from other groups of musicians?

Staff Benda Bilili is a group of musicians from Kinshasa, Democratic Republic of Congo (DRC). They live on the streets of the city. The four original group members are all disabled and move around on homemade tricycles. The group was founded by guitar players Papa Ricky Likabu and Coco Ngambali. Other musicians refused to play with them because they couldn't dance. Later, a street kid, Roger Landu, joined them. He made his own musical instrument from a fish can, a piece of wood, and one guitar string – nothing more.

The group's music is classic Congolese rumba mixed with reggae and rhythm 'n' blues. Their lyrics contain a message to street people and disabled people: Be very strong. Papa Ricky believes that the only real handicaps are in the mind, not the body. He says the group's main musical influences come from the street: "We sleep there, eat there, rehearse there." They also play there. Every evening, the group performs in front of an audience near Kinshasa Zoo.

In 2004, two French filmmakers were working in the DRC when, by chance, they heard Staff Benda Bilili's music. They loved it so much that they spent the next five years making a documentary film about the group. In 2009, Staff Benda Bilili's first CD was released. It's called *Très Très Fort*, which means "very very strong." The group won the WOMEX (World Music Expo) Artist Award. Then, in 2010, the documentary *Benda Bilili!* was screened at the Cannes Film Festival, and the group played on the opening night.

Staff Benda Bilili wants to use its worldwide success to raise awareness about the problems of street people in Kinshasa and around the world.

A Read the article. Find the words in *italics* below in the article. Then match each word with its meaning.

.... 1. *disabled*   a. unexpectedly
.... 2. *lyrics*   b. make people think
.... 3. *handicaps*   c. things that make it hard to do what you want
.... 4. *rehearse*   d. words of a song
.... 5. *by chance*   e. unable to walk or move easily
.... 6. *raise awareness*   f. practice before performing in front of an audience

B Answer these questions. Then compare with a partner.

1. Where do the members of Staff Benda Bilili live? ....
2. Why do they use tricycles? ....
3. What kind of music do they play? ....
4. How did they become famous? ....
5. What message do they want to tell the world? ....

C **PAIR WORK** Discuss people you know who had a lot of problems and then became very successful.

Units 11–12 Progress check

SELF-ASSESSMENT

How well can you do these things? Check (✓) the boxes.

I can	Very well	OK	A little
Give information about books, movies, songs, etc. (Ex. 1)	☐	☐	☐
Understand information about countries (Ex. 2)	☐	☐	☐
Describe a situation (Ex. 3)	☐	☐	☐
Ask and answer questions about past events (Ex. 4, 5)	☐	☐	☐
Ask and answer questions about recent activities (Ex. 5)	☐	☐	☐

1 SPEAKING *Right or wrong?*

A List six books, movies, songs, albums, or other popular works.
Then write one *who* question for each of the six items.

> The *X-Men* movies
> Who played Wolverine in the *X-Men* movies?

B **PAIR WORK** Take turns asking your questions.
Use the passive with *by* to answer.

A: Who played Wolverine in the *X-Men* movies?
B: I think Wolverine was played by Hugh Jackman.

2 LISTENING *Facts about Spain*

A ▶ Listen to people on a game show answer questions about Spain.
What are the answers? Complete the chart.

1. Currency	4. A popular sport	
2. Country to the west	5. Two main crops	
3. Capital	6. Two industries	

B ▶ Listen again. Keep score. How much money does each contestant have?

GAME *Sentence-making competition*

GROUP WORK Use the passive to write details about these situations.
Then compare with the class. Which group wrote the most sentences?

| Your roommate cleaned the apartment. | There was a big storm yesterday. | Someone broke into your house last night. |

| The dishes were done. | The airport was closed. | The window was broken. |

 ## ROLE PLAY *Alibis*

> A famous painting has been stolen from a local museum. It disappeared last Sunday afternoon between 12 P.M. and 4 P.M.

Student A: Student B suspects you stole the painting. Make up an alibi. Take notes on what you were doing that day. Then answer Student B's questions.

Student B: You are a police detective. You think Student A stole the painting. Add two questions to the notebook. Then ask Student A the questions.

Change roles and try the role play again.

> Where were you last Sunday?
>
> Did you eat lunch? Who was with you?
>
> What were you wearing that day?
>
> What were you doing between noon and 4 p.m.?
>
> Was anyone with you?
>
> _____
>
> _____

 ## DISCUSSION *Really? How interesting.*

A GROUP WORK What interesting things can you find out about your classmates? Ask these questions and others of your own.

Have you been doing anything exciting recently?
Are you studying anything right now? How long have you been studying it?
Have you met anyone interesting lately?
Who is your best friend? How did you meet?
Where were you living ten years ago? Did you like it there? What do you remember about it?

useful expressions
Really?
I didn't know that!
Oh, I see.
I had no idea.
Wow! Tell me more.

B CLASS ACTIVITY Tell the class the most interesting thing you learned.

WHAT'S NEXT?

Look at your Self-assessment again. Do you need to review anything?

13 Good book, terrible movie!

1 SNAPSHOT

Movie Trivia

- **Batman** (1989)   The role of Batman was played by Michael Keaton. In later movies, it was played by Val Kilmer, George Clooney, and Christian Bale.
- **Titanic** (1997)   The movie cost $200 million to make. The Titanic itself cost about $135 million to build.
- **Pirates of the Caribbean: The Curse of the Black Pearl** (2003) Keira Knightley nearly missed the audition because of a traffic jam.
- **Harry Potter and the Order of the Phoenix** (2007) This is the longest book and the shortest movie in the series.
- **Paranormal Activity** (2007)   This movie only cost $15,000 to make, but it made $9.1 million in its first week.
- **Avatar** (2009)   The special effects were so expensive that director James Cameron had to wait ten years to make the movie.
- **The Three Stooges** (2012)   Jim Carrey, Sean Penn, and Benicio del Toro were originally cast in the film, but all three dropped out.

Source: www.imdb.com

Which of the movie trivia do you find most interesting?
Do you know any other movie trivia?
Which of the movies have you seen? Did you enjoy them?

2 CONVERSATION   *What's playing?*

A ▶ Listen and practice.

Roger: Do you want to see a movie tonight?
Carol: Hmm. Maybe. What's playing?
Roger: How about the new *Star Trek* film? I hear it's really exciting.
Carol: Actually, the last one was boring.
Roger: What about the movie based on Stephen King's new novel?
Carol: I don't know. His books are usually fascinating, but I don't like horror movies.
Roger: Well, what do you want to see?
Carol: I'm interested in the new Sandra Bullock movie. It looks good.
Roger: That's fine with me. She's a wonderful actress.

B ▶ Listen to the rest of the conversation. What happens next? What do they decide to do?

Sandra Bullock

86

3 GRAMMAR FOCUS

> ### Participles as adjectives ▶
>
> **Present participles**
> Stephen King's books are **fascinating**.
> The last *Star Trek* film was **boring**.
> The new Sandra Bullock movie
>   sounds **interesting**.
>
> **Past participles**
> I'm **fascinated** by Stephen King's books.
> I was **bored** by the last *Star Trek* film.
> I'm **interested** in the new Sandra
>   Bullock movie.

A Complete these sentences. Then compare with a partner.

1. Matt Damon is an .... actor. (amaze)
2. I find animated films .... (amuse)
3. I'm not .... in science fiction movies. (interest)
4. I'm .... by watching television. (bore)
5. The final *Twilight* book was .... (excite)
6. I'm .... by J.R.R. Tolkien's novels. (fascinate)
7. It's .... that horror movies are so popular. (surprise)

Matt Damon

B PAIR WORK Complete the description below with the correct form of these words.

| amaze | annoy | confuse | disgust | embarrass | shock |

I had a terrible time at the movies last weekend. First, my ticket cost $15. I was really
.... by the price. By mistake, I gave the cashier two $5 bills instead of
a ten and a five. I was a little .... Then there was trash all over the theater.
The mess was .... The people behind me were talking during the movie,
which was .... The story was hard to follow. I always find thrillers
so .... I liked the special effects, though. They were .... !

4 WORD POWER Opinions

A PAIR WORK Complete the chart with synonyms from the list.

absurd	dumb	marvelous	silly
bizarre	fabulous	odd	terrible
disgusting	fantastic	outstanding	unusual
dreadful	horrible	ridiculous	weird

Awful	Wonderful	Stupid	Strange
....	....	....	....
....	....	....	....
....	....	....	....
....	....	....	....

B GROUP WORK Share your opinions about a movie, an actor,
an actress, a TV show, and a book. Use words from part A.

5 LISTENING *How did you like it?*

A Listen to people talk about books, movies, and TV programs. Which ones do you think they would recommend?

B Listen again. Check (✓) the adjective that best describes what the people say about each one.

1. ☐ fascinating **2.** ☐ wonderful **3.** ☐ boring **4.** ☐ ridiculous
   ☐ silly   ☐ odd   ☐ terrific   ☐ interesting
   ☐ strange   ☐ boring   ☐ dreadful   ☐ exciting

6 PRONUNCIATION *Emphatic stress*

A Listen and practice. Notice how stress and a higher pitch are used to express strong opinions.

● That was terrible!   ● He was amazing!   ● That's fascinating!

B **PAIR WORK** Write four statements using these words. Then take turns reading them. Pay attention to emphatic stress.

dreadful   fantastic   horrible   ridiculous

7 DISCUSSION *Let's go to the movies!*

A **PAIR WORK** Take turns asking and answering these questions and others of your own.

What kinds of movies are you interested in? Why?
What kinds of movies do you find boring?
Who are your favorite actors and actresses? Why?
Are there actors or actresses you don't like?
What's the worst movie you've ever seen?
What are your three favorite movies in
   English? Why?
Are there any outstanding movies playing now?

A: What kinds of movies are you interested in?
B: I love action movies.
A: Really? Why is that?
B: They're exciting! What about you?
A: I think action movies are kind of silly. I prefer . . .

B **GROUP WORK** Compare your information. Whose taste in movies is most like yours?

NOW SHOWING on DVD
COMEDIES
THRILLERS
DRAMA
MYSTERIES
ACTION / ADVENTURE
SCIENCE FICTION
Romance
CLASSICS
DOCUMENTARIES
HORROR
ANIMATION

8 PERSPECTIVES *It's about . . .*

A ⊙ Listen to people talk about some of their Hollywood favorites.
Can you guess the actress, actor, or movie each person is describing?

1. This action movie came out in
   2010 and stars Leonardo DiCaprio
   as a thief who is able to steal
   information from people's minds.
   It's kind of confusing, but the special
   effects are amazing.

2. He's an actor who often plays
   unusual characters. He's fantastic as the
   Mad Hatter in *Alice in Wonderland* and
   Captain Jack Sparrow in the *Pirates of
   the Caribbean* movies.

3. It's a science fiction movie that
   was directed by James Cameron.
   It's a beautiful film that takes place
   on the moon Pandora in the year
   2154. It's a story about the clash of
   cultures and civilizations.

4. She's an actress who is excellent
   in both dramas and comedies.
   I loved her in *Mamma Mia!* and
   The Iron Lady. I haven't seen a lot
   of her earlier movies, though.

B Do you like the people and movies described in part A? What else do you know about them?

9 GRAMMAR FOCUS

Relative pronouns for people and things ⊙

Use who or that for people.
He's an actor. He often plays
   unusual characters.
He's an actor **who/that** often plays
   unusual characters.

Use which or that for things.
It's a movie. It stars Leonardo DiCaprio.

It's a movie **which/that** stars
   Leonardo DiCaprio.

A Combine the sentences using relative pronouns. Then compare with a partner.

1. *Super Mario Galaxy 2* is a video game. It's fun for all ages.
2. Jodie Foster is an actress. She began her career at age three.
3. Ben Affleck is an actor. He's also a director.
4. *The Lorax* is a film. It was adapted from a children's book.
5. Jaden Smith is an actor. He's the son of Will Smith.
6. Dan Brown writes books. They're hard to put down.
7. *Wicked* is a Broadway musical. It's been very successful.
8. Beyoncé is a singer. She's acted in several films.

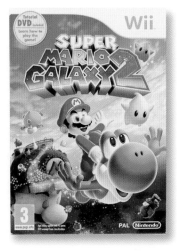

B **PAIR WORK** Complete these sentences. Then compare
your information around the class.

1. Cameron Diaz is an actress . . .
2. *Toy Story 3* is a movie . . .
3. Justin Bieber is a singer . . .
4. *The Simpsons* is a TV show . . .

10 INTERCHANGE 13 *Famous faces*

What do you know about movies and TV shows? Go to Interchange 13 on page 127.

11 SPEAKING A new TV show

A **PAIR WORK** A TV studio is looking for ideas for a new TV show. Brainstorm possible ideas and agree on an idea. Make brief notes.

What kind of TV show is it?
What's it about?
Who are the main characters?
Who will it appeal to?

B **CLASS ACTIVITY** Tell the class about your TV show.

"Our TV show is a detective story. It's about two secret agents who are chasing an alien from another planet. There are two main characters. . . ."

12 LISTENING A night at the movies

A ⊙ Listen to two critics talk about a new movie. What do they like or not like about it? Rate each item in the chart from 1 to 3.

	Acting	Story	Music	Special effects
Pauline	....	....	....	....
Colin	....	....	....	....

Ratings
1 = didn't like it
2 = OK
3 = liked it very much

B ⊙ Look at the chart in part A. Guess how many stars each critic gave the movie. Then listen to the critics give their ratings.

★ poor   ★★ fair   ★★★ good   ★★★★ excellent

13 WRITING A movie review

A **PAIR WORK** Choose a movie you both have seen and discuss it. Then write a review of it.

What was the movie about?
What did you like about it?
What didn't you like about it?
How was the acting?
How would you rate it?

B **CLASS ACTIVITY** Read your review to the class. Who else has seen the movie? Do they agree with your review?

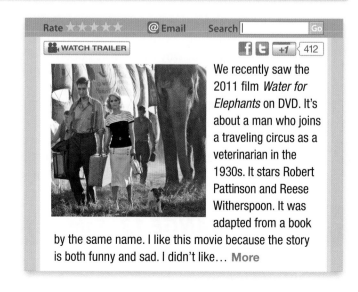

Rate ★★★★★   @Email   Search [   ] Go

WATCH TRAILER   f t +1 412

We recently saw the 2011 film *Water for Elephants* on DVD. It's about a man who joins a traveling circus as a veterinarian in the 1930s. It stars Robert Pattinson and Reese Witherspoon. It was adapted from a book by the same name. I like this movie because the story is both funny and sad. I didn't like… **More**

SPECIAL EFFECTS

Scan the article. What is the most important change in special effects?

1 Nowadays, almost anything can happen in the movies. Dinosaurs rule the world, people fly, and aliens attack spacecraft. But how is it all possible?

2 Special effects started long before the movies. For centuries, magicians performed in the streets, usually in markets and fairs. They did card tricks and things like making rabbits "disappear." In the early nineteenth century, before the invention of electricity, actors in theaters were highlighted by limelights. Sometime later, a lighting technique called "Pepper's ghost" was used to make ghosts "appear" on stage. Audiences were thrilled.

3 Motion pictures began in the 1890s, but there was no sound. They were "silent movies." "Talkies" were first shown in the 1920s. Later, color films gradually replaced black-and-white ones.

4 From the 1950s to the 1980s, special effects became more and more fantastic. Experts in robotics, computers, engineering, and other fields were employed by filmmakers. However, the biggest development in special effects came with computer-generated imagery (CGI) in the 1990s. *Jurassic Park* (1993) had full shots of dinosaurs using CGI. *Titanic* (1997) used CGI for shots on board the ship and very small models to show underwater shots of the ship.

5 More recently, *Avatar* (2009) used 60 percent CGI and 40 percent live action. It was the first film to be shot entirely with a 3-D camera. It shows totally believable scenes of humans and aliens on the moon Pandora.

6 Special effects in movies are both a science and an art. Computer technology and human imagination come together to bring stories to life. They make science fiction and action movies much more exciting to watch, and audiences love them.

A Read the article. Then number these sentences from 1 (first event) to 9 (last event).

.... a. Silent movies were shown.
.... b. CGI was developed.
.... c. Limelights were used in theaters.
.... d. CGI was used to show dinosaurs.
.... e. Talkies began to replace silent movies.
.... f. Street magicians performed tricks.
.... g. Color movies were shown.
.... h. Small models and CGI were used in *Titanic*.
.... i. The first full movie was made with a 3-D camera.

B Where do these sentences belong? Write the number of the paragraph where each sentence should go.

.... a. It used the movie format IMAX 3-D.
.... b. Movies also show amazing things like meteors hitting the Earth.
.... c. This meant audiences could see the stage more clearly.
.... d. Models were used for shots of parts of dinosaurs.
.... e. Even if special effects are often very expensive, they are good for business.
.... f. One of the first films with sound was *The Jazz Singer*.

C **PAIR WORK** What movie do you think has the best special effects? Why do you like them?

14 So that's what it means!

Popular Emoticons

:-)	I'm happy.			#-)	I'm sleepy.
:-(	I'm sad.	(:+(	That was scary!	:-9	That was delicious!
}:[	I'm angry.	:-X	I can't talk about it.	:-~(	I have a terrible cold.
;-)	Just kidding!	:-/	Really? That can't be right!	:-&	I don't know what to say!
:-D	That's funny!	:-O	I'm surprised!	:-|	I'm so bored.

Source: www.computeruser.com

Do people in your country use emoticons? Do you?
What other emoticons can you use to communicate these ideas?
What other emoticons do you know?

2 WORD POWER *Feelings and gestures*

A What is this man doing in each picture? Match each description with a picture. Then compare with a partner.

1. He's biting his nails. ....
2. He's rolling his eyes. ....
3. He's scratching his head. ....
4. He's tapping his foot. ....
5. He's twirling his hair. ....
6. He's wrinkling his nose. ....

 **a**    **b**    **c**

 **d**    **e**

B **GROUP WORK** Use the pictures in part A and these adjectives to describe how the man is feeling.

annoyed	confused	embarrassed	frustrated	irritated
bored	disgusted	exhausted	impatient	nervous

"In the first picture, he's twirling his hair. He looks nervous."

 **f**

3 CONVERSATION *Have you met Raj?*

A ▶ Listen and practice.

Ron: Have you met Raj, the student from India?

Emily: No, I haven't.

Ron: Well, he seems really nice, but there's one thing I noticed. He moves his head from side to side when you talk to him. You know, like this.

Emily: Maybe it means he doesn't understand you.

Ron: No, I don't think so.

Emily: Or it could mean he doesn't agree with you.

Peter: Actually, people from India sometimes move their heads from side to side when they agree with you.

Ron: Oh, so that's what it means!

B ▶ Now listen to Raj talk to his friend. What does he find unusual about the way people in North America communicate?

4 GRAMMAR FOCUS

Modals and adverbs ▶

Modals	**Adverbs**
It **might/may** mean he doesn't understand you.	**Maybe/Perhaps** it means he doesn't understand you.
It **could** mean he doesn't agree with you.	It **possibly/probably** means he doesn't agree with you.
That **must** mean he agrees with you.	That **definitely** means he agrees with you.

PAIR WORK What do these gestures mean? Take turns making statements about each gesture using the meanings in the box.

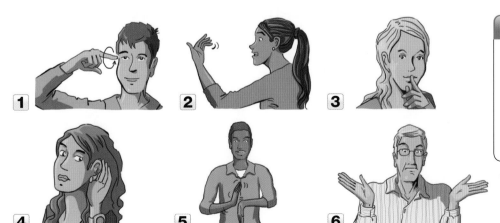

possible meanings
I don't know.
Be quiet.
I'm finished.
That sounds crazy!
I can't hear you.
Come here.

A: What do you think the first gesture means?

B: It probably means . . . , or it might mean . . .

5 SPEAKING *What does it mean?*

A **PAIR WORK** Imagine you are in a foreign country and you don't speak the language. Think of gestures to communicate these meanings.

Go away.	I don't understand.
Help!	It's delicious.
Please repeat.	How much does this cost?
I'm lost.	Someone stole my wallet.
I'm hungry.	Where's the bathroom?

B **CLASS ACTIVITY** What else could your gestures mean? For each gesture you acted out in part A, think of one more possible meaning.

A: That probably means "go away," but it might also mean you don't like something.
B: It could also mean . . .

6 PRONUNCIATION *Pitch*

A Listen and practice. Notice how pitch is used to express certainty or doubt.

	Certain	**Uncertain**
A: Do you think her gesture means "go away"?	B: Definitely.	B: Probably.
A: Do you understand what her gesture means?	B: Absolutely.	B: Maybe.

B **PAIR WORK** Take turns asking yes/no questions. Respond by using *absolutely, definitely, maybe, probably,* and your own information. Pay attention to pitch.

7 INTERCHANGE 14 *What's going on?*

Interpret people's body language. Go to Interchange 14 on page 128.

8 PERSPECTIVES *Signs*

A ▶ What do you think these international signs mean? Listen and match each sign with the correct meaning.

1. .... 2. .... 3. .... 4. .... 5. .... 6. .... 7. .... 8. ....

a. You can camp here.
b. You aren't allowed to take photos here.
c. You have to fasten your seat belts.
d. You can recycle this item.

e. You have to wear a hard hat to enter this area.
f. You can't drink the water here. It's not safe.
g. You have to keep your dog on a leash here.
h. You've got to take off your shoes here.

B PAIR WORK Where might you see the signs in part A? Give two suggestions for each one.

"You might see this one at a national park or . . ."

9 GRAMMAR FOCUS

Permission, obligation, and prohibition ▶

Permission	Obligation	Prohibition
You **can** camp here.	You **have to** camp here.	You **can't** camp here.
You**'re allowed to** take off your shoes.	You**'ve got to** take off your shoes.	You **aren't allowed to** take off your shoes.

A Match these school rules with the correct sign. Then compare with a partner.

1. Lock your bikes in the bike rack. ....
2. No eating or drinking in the classroom. ....
3. No playing ball in the hallway. ....
4. Keep the classroom door closed. ....
5. No listening to music. ....
6. Throw trash in the wastebasket. ....
7. No cell phones. ....
8. Turn out the lights when leaving. ....

a   b   c   d

e   f   g   h

B PAIR WORK Use the language in the grammar box to take turns talking about each sign.

A: This first sign means you aren't allowed to eat or drink in the classroom.
B: Yes, I think you're right. And the second one means you have to . . .

10 DISCUSSION *Rules and regulations*

A PAIR WORK How many rules can you think of for each of these places?

on an airplane	in an art museum	on a bus or subway
in a library	in a movie theater	at work

"On an airplane, you have to wear your seat belt when the plane is taking off and landing."

B GROUP WORK Share your ideas. Why do you think these rules exist? Have you ever broken any of them? What happened?

11 LISTENING *Sign language*

A ▶ Listen to three conversations about driving. Check (✓) True or False for each statement.

	True	False
1. The man hasn't had a parking ticket lately.	☐	☐
Parking isn't allowed there during working hours.	☐	☐
The fine for parking is $16.	☐	☐
2. The woman is driving faster than the speed limit.	☐	☐
There are other cars in her lane.	☐	☐
The lane is reserved for buses and taxis.	☐	☐
3. The other drivers are flashing their lights.	☐	☐
He's driving with his lights on.	☐	☐
The other drivers are giving him a warning.	☐	☐

B ▶ Listen again. Which of the drivers did something wrong?

12 WRITING *A list of rules*

A GROUP WORK Discuss the rules that currently exist at your school. How many can you think of? Are they all good rules?

B GROUP WORK Think of four new rules that you feel would be a good idea. Work together to write brief explanations of why each is necessary.

> 1. You aren't allowed to chew gum in class because it may bother other students.
>
> 2. You can be late, but you have to come in quietly so you don't disturb the lesson.
>
> 3. You have to pay a small fine if your cell phone rings in class because . . .

C CLASS ACTIVITY Share your lists. Vote on the best new rules.

Pearls of Wisdom

**Look at these proverbs and the pictures below.
Then match each proverb with a picture.**

a *A bird in the hand is worth two in the bush.*

b *One person's meat is another one's poison.*

c *Don't count your chickens before they hatch.*

d *Money doesn't grow on trees.*

1 **Why do people use proverbs?** Many people love proverbs for their wisdom. Others enjoy the images in proverbs. But proverbs are most impressive because they express a lot of information in just a few words. A good proverb quickly sums up ideas that are sometimes hard to express. And the person listening immediately understands the message.

2 **Where do proverbs come from?** Proverbs come from two main places – ordinary people and famous people. These two sources are not always distinct. Common and popular wisdom has often been used by famous people.

And something said or written down by a well-known person has often been borrowed by the common man. For example, "Bad news travels fast" probably comes from the experience of housewives. However, "All's well that ends well" was written by William Shakespeare.

3 **What do proverbs tell us?** Proverbs are used everywhere in the world. If you can understand a culture's proverbs, you can better understand the culture itself. There are many different ways that we use proverbs in daily life. Here are some examples of what proverbs can do:

Give advice
Meaning: Something you have is better than something you might get.

Give a warning
Meaning: Don't plan on a successful outcome until it actually happens.

Teach a lesson
Meaning: It's not easy to get money.

Express a common truth
Meaning: What one person loves, another person may hate.

A Read the article. Then find these sentences in the article. Decide whether each sentence is the main idea or a supporting idea in that paragraph. Check (✓) the correct boxes.

	Main idea	Supporting idea
1. Many people love proverbs for their wisdom. (par. 1)	☐	☐
2. But proverbs are most . . . just a few words. (par. 1)	☐	☐
3. Proverbs come from . . . and famous people. (par. 2)	☐	☐
4. If you can understand . . . the culture itself. (par. 3)	☐	☐
5. There are many . . . proverbs in daily life. (par. 3)	☐	☐

B **CLASS ACTIVITY** Think of an interesting proverb from your country. What does it mean? Tell it to the class in English.

Units 13–14 Progress check

SELF-ASSESSMENT

How well can you do these things? Check (✓) the boxes.

I can	Very well	OK	A little
Ask about and express opinions and emotions (Ex. 1, 4, 5)	☐	☐	☐
Describe people and things (Ex. 2)	☐	☐	☐
Understand speculations and recognize emotions (Ex. 3, 4)	☐	☐	☐
Speculate about things when I'm not sure (Ex. 3, 4)	☐	☐	☐
Describe rules and laws: permission, obligation, and prohibition (Ex. 5)	☐	☐	☐

1 SURVEY *Entertainment opinions*

A Complete the first column of the survey with your opinions.

	Me	My classmate
A confusing movie		
A boring TV show		
A shocking news story		
A fascinating book		
An interesting celebrity		
A singer you are amazed by		
A song you are annoyed by		

B CLASS ACTIVITY Go around the class and find someone who has the same opinions. Write a classmate's name only once.

"I thought *Inception* was a confusing movie. What about you?"

2 ROLE PLAY *Movie recommendations*

Student A: Invite Student B to a movie. Suggest two films.
Then answer your partner's questions.
Start like this: *Do you want to see a movie?*

Student B: Student A invites you to a movie. Find out more about the movie. Then accept or refuse the invitation.

Change roles and try the role play again.

3 LISTENING *That's how I feel!*

A ▶ Listen to some people talking. Write what each person is talking about.

1. .... 2. .... 3. .... 4. ....

B ▶ Listen again. What does each person mean? Check (✓) the best answer.

1. ☐ He is confused.
   ☐ He is nervous.

2. ☐ She enjoyed it.
   ☐ She hated it.

3. ☐ He didn't understand it.
   ☐ He thought it was interesting.

4. ☐ She is frustrated.
   ☐ She is bored.

4 GAME *Charades*

A Think of two emotions or ideas you can communicate with gestures. Write them on separate cards.

> I'm tired of waiting.

B GROUP WORK Shuffle your cards together. Then take turns picking cards and acting out the meanings with gestures. The student who guesses correctly goes next.

A: That probably means you're bored.
B: No.
C: It could mean you're impatient.
B: You're getting closer. . . .

5 DISCUSSION *What's the law?*

GROUP WORK Read these laws from the United States. What do you think about them? Are they the same or different in your country?

- You're allowed to vote when you turn 18.
- In some states, you can get married when you're 16.
- You have to wear a seat belt in the front seat of a car.
- Young men don't have to serve in the military.
- You aren't allowed to keep certain wild animals as pets.
- In some states, you can't drive faster than 65 miles per hour (about 100 kph).
- You have to have a passport to enter the country.

A: In the U.S., you're allowed to vote when you turn 18.
B: That's surprising! In my country, we *have* to vote when we're 18.
C: And in my country, we *can't* vote until we're 20.

WHAT'S NEXT?

Look at your Self-assessment again. Do you need to review anything?

15 What would you do?

1 SNAPSHOT

The Morning News

| HOME | CURRENT ISSUE | ARCHIVES | WEB EXTRAS | RADIO | CONTACT US | SUBSCRIBE |

Stories of Honesty

Businessman returns $750,000 to owner – and is thanked with a brief phone call
READ MORE ➕

Athlete admits to cheating – confesses that he "just wanted to win"
READ MORE ➕

Taxi driver returns computer – drives miles to give laptop back to passenger
READ MORE ➕

Golfer admits using illegal ball by mistake – but is still disqualified from game
READ MORE ➕

Student uses detective work to find owner of gold jewelry
READ MORE ➕

Fan returns soccer star's lucky T-shirt – player gives him $1,000 reward
READ MORE ➕

Sources: www.geardiary.com; http://sports.espn.go.com; *Los Angeles Times*

Do you know any other stories like these?
Have you ever found anything valuable? What did you do?
Do you think that people who return lost things should get a reward?

2 CONVERSATION *If I found $750,000, . . .*

A ▶ Listen and practice.

Phil: Look at this. Some guy found $750,000! He returned it, and the owner simply thanked him with a phone call.

Pat: You're kidding! If I found $750,000, I wouldn't return it so fast.

Phil: Why? What would you do?

Pat: Well, I'd go out and start spending it. I could buy lots of nice clothes and jewelry.

Phil: Someone might also find out about it. And then you could go to jail.

Pat: Hmm. You've got a point there.

B ▶ Listen to the rest of the conversation. What would Phil do if he found $750,000?

3 GRAMMAR FOCUS

> **Unreal conditional sentences with if clauses** ⊙
>
> | Imaginary situation (simple past) | Possible consequence (would, could, or might + verb) |
> |---|---|
> | If I **found** $750,000, | I **would spend** it. |
> | | I **wouldn't return** it so fast. |
> | | I **could buy** lots of nice clothes and jewelry. |
> | | I **might go** to the police. |
>
> What **would** you **do if** you **found** $750,000?

A Complete these conversations. Then compare with a partner.

1. A: If you .... (have) three months to travel, where .... you .... (go)?
   B: Oh, that's easy! I .... (fly) to Europe. I've always wanted to go there.

2. A: If your doctor .... (tell) you to get more exercise, which sport .... you .... (choose)?
   B: I'm not sure, but I .... (go) jogging two or three times a week.

3. A: What .... you .... (do) if your teacher .... (give) you an A by mistake?
   B: Of course I .... (say) something right away.

4. A: .... you .... (break) into your house if you .... (lock) yourself out?
   B: If I .... (not have) another key, I .... (ask) a neighbor for help.

5. A: If your friend .... (want) to marry someone you didn't trust, ... you .... (say) something?
   B: No, I .... (not say) anything. I .... (mind) my own business.

6. A: What .... you .... (do) if you .... (see) your favorite movie star on the street?
   B: I .... (not be) shy! I .... (ask) for a photo and an autograph.

B PAIR WORK Take turns asking the questions in part A.
Answer with your own information.

4 LISTENING *Tough predicaments*

A ⊙ Listen to three people talk about predicaments. Number them from 1 to 3 in the order they are discussed.

Predicament	Suggestions
☐ Two people were fighting in the street.	....
☐ A friend lost all her money while traveling.	....
☐ A friend has a serious shopping problem.	....

B ⊙ Listen again. What suggestions do the people give for each predicament? Take notes. Which is the best suggestion?

5 INTERCHANGE 15 *Do the right thing!*

What would you do in some difficult situations? Go to Interchange 15 on page 130.

6 WORD POWER *Opposites*

A Find nine pairs of opposites in this list. Complete the chart.
Then compare with a partner.

✓ accept   borrow   dislike   find   lose   remember
admit   deny   divorce   forget   marry   save
agree   disagree   enjoy   lend   ✓ refuse   spend

accept	≠	refuse	....	≠	....	....	≠	....
....	≠	....	....	≠	....	....	≠	....
....	≠	....	....	≠	....	....	≠	....

B PAIR WORK Choose four pairs of opposites. Write sentences using each pair.

> I can never save money because I spend it all on clothes.

7 PERSPECTIVES *I felt terrible.*

A ▶ Listen to people talk about recent predicaments.
Then check (✓) the best suggestion for each one.

> **"What a disaster! I spilled juice on my parents' new couch. They weren't home, so I just turned the cushions over. What should I have done?"**
>
> ☐ You should have told them about it.
>
> ☐ You should have cleaned it immediately.
>
> ☐ You should have offered to buy them a new couch.

> **"I forgot my best friend's birthday. I felt terrible, so I sent him a text to apologize. What would you have done?"**
>
> ☐ I would have called him right away.
>
> ☐ I would have sent him a nice birthday present.
>
> ☐ I would have invited him out for a meal.

B PAIR WORK Compare with a partner. Do you agree with each other?

8 GRAMMAR FOCUS

Past modals ▶

Use would have or should have + past participle to give opinions or suggestions about actions in the past.

What **should** I **have done**?

You **should have told** them about it.
You **shouldn't have hidden** it.

What **would** you **have done**?

I **would have called** him.
I **wouldn't have sent** him a text.

A Complete these conversations. Then practice with a partner.

1. A: The cashier gave me too much change. What should I have .... (do)?
   B: You should have .... (say) something. You shouldn't have .... (take) the money.

2. A: I ignored an email from someone I don't like. What would you have .... (do)?
   B: I would have .... (reply) to the person. It just takes a minute!

3. A: I was watching a good movie when my phone rang. What should I have .... (do)?
   B: You should have .... (take) the call and .... (tell) the person you'd call back later.

4. A: We left all our trash at the campsite. What would you have .... (do)?
   B: I would have .... (take) it with me and .... (throw) it away later.

B Read the situations below. What would have been the best thing to do? Choose suggestions. Then compare with a partner.

Situations

1. The teacher borrowed my favorite book and spilled coffee all over it. ....
2. I saw a classmate cheating on an exam. So I wrote her an email about it. ....
3. A friend of mine always has messy hair. So I gave him a comb for his birthday. ....
4. I hit someone's car when I was leaving a parking lot. Luckily, no one saw me. ....
5. My aunt gave me a wool sweater. I can't wear wool, so I gave it back. ....

Suggestions

a. You should have spoken to him about it.
b. I would have spoken to the teacher about it.
c. I would have waited for the owner to return.
d. I wouldn't have said anything.
e. You should have warned her not to do it again.
f. You should have left a note for the owner.
g. I would have told her that I prefer something else.
h. You should have exchanged it for something else.

C GROUP WORK Make another suggestion for each situation in part B.

9 PRONUNCIATION Reduction of have

A ▶ Listen and practice. Notice how **have** is reduced in these sentences.

/əv/
What would you have done?

/əv/
I would have told the truth.

B PAIR WORK Practice the conversations in Exercise 8, part A, again. Use the reduced form of **have**.

10 LISTENING *I'm calling about . . .*

A ▶ Listen to people calling Dr. Hilda, a counselor on a radio talk show. Complete the chart.

	Problem	What the caller did
Caller 1	....	....
Caller 2	....	....
Caller 3	....	....

B ▶ Listen again. According to Dr. Hilda, what should each caller have done?

C GROUP WORK Do you agree with Dr. Hilda? What would you have done?

11 SPEAKING *I shouldn't have . . .*

A Look at the five situations below. Think about the past month and write down an example for each situation.

1. something you shouldn't have done
2. something you should have done
3. something you shouldn't have said
4. somewhere you shouldn't have gone
5. someone you should have emailed or called

B GROUP WORK Talk about each situation in part A.

"I spent $50 on a T-shirt. I shouldn't have bought it. I don't even like it now."

12 WRITING *A letter to an advice columnist*

Write a letter to an advice columnist about a real or imaginary problem. Put your letters on the wall and choose one to write a reply to.

> Dear Dr. Hilda,
>
> I let a friend borrow my laptop, and now it's not working very well. I took it to a repair shop, and they said it would be very expensive to fix. When I asked my friend to help me pay for the repair, she refused. Now she won't even speak to me! What did I do wrong? What should I have done?
> Thanks for your help!
>
> Kevin

The Advice Circle

Login/Join

Search [   ] Go   Tweet 12   f Like

Skim the three posts on the message board. What problem does each writer have?

| Health | Parenting | Education | Lifestyle | **Relationships** |

Terry — Someone told me that my brother's girlfriend was dating another guy. I told my brother and he then decided to confront her with the story. They had an argument and, although she denied the rumor, they broke up. Now it turns out that the rumor wasn't true, and my brother isn't speaking to me.   Posts: **11**

Pixie — You really learned a lesson, didn't you? You shouldn't have listened to gossip. Now you have to repair the damage. Apologize and hope that he will forgive and forget!   Posts: **14**   Hide Post

Lola — Don't blame yourself. You sincerely tried your best. But, frankly, I wouldn't have acted so quickly. I would have waited to see what happened. Try talking to him – and good luck!   Posts: **7**   Hide Post

Linda — My son is 23 and still lives at home. He finished college last year, but I really don't think he's trying to get a job. Meanwhile, I've been cooking his meals and doing his laundry.   Posts: **21**

Too Bad — You're making it too easy for him to stay home. Be firm and tell him he has to find a job and get his own place. He's old enough to take care of himself.   Posts: **17**   Hide Post

Poodle — You're his mother, and family is family. It's hard to find a job if you have no experience. And don't you have to cook for yourself? Don't complain about your son.   Posts: **3**   Hide Post

Robin — I saw my friend's brother at the beach with some of his friends. It wasn't a holiday, so I think he was skipping school. Should I tell my friend?   Posts: **15**

Zeb — I would suggest you keep your mouth shut. Let them work things out for themselves. If you say something, you could damage your friendship with both of them.   Posts: **27**   Hide Post

Speedy — What are you waiting for? You should tell your friend right now, and tell her mom, too! The only way to solve your dilemma is to be 100% honest.   Posts: **10**   Hide Post

A Read the message board. Match the name and the advice.

1. Pixie ....   a. Be honest.
2. Lola ....   b. Say nothing.
3. Too Bad ....   c. Be firm.
4. Poodle ....   d. Apologize.
5. Zeb ....   e. Talk to him.
6. Speedy ....   f. Don't complain.

B Find the words in *italics* below in the message board. Then match each one with its meaning.

.... 1. *confront*   a. make a fresh start
.... 2. *forgive and forget* b. strong and determined
.... 3. *firm*   c. a difficult problem
.... 4. *dilemma*   d. discuss in a strong, direct way

C **PAIR WORK** Which advice do you agree or disagree with? What advice would you give?

16 What's your excuse?

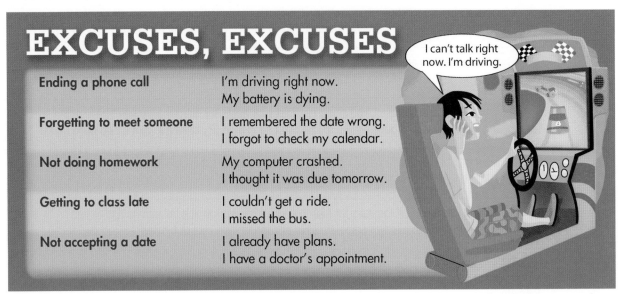

EXCUSES, EXCUSES

Ending a phone call	I'm driving right now. My battery is dying.
Forgetting to meet someone	I remembered the date wrong. I forgot to check my calendar.
Not doing homework	My computer crashed. I thought it was due tomorrow.
Getting to class late	I couldn't get a ride. I missed the bus.
Not accepting a date	I already have plans. I have a doctor's appointment.

I can't talk right now. I'm driving.

Source: Based on www.answers.yahoo.com

Have you ever heard any of these excuses? Have you ever used any of them?
Which are good excuses? Which are bad excuses?
What other excuses can you make for not accepting an invitation?

2 PERSPECTIVES *Who said it?*

A ▶ Who do you think made these requests? Listen and match.

1. He asked me to play my music more quietly.	**a.** my doctor
2. She told me not to stay out past midnight.	**b.** my coach
3. She said to drink at least six glasses of water a day.	**c.** my friend
4. He said not to be late for practice again.	**d.** my neighbor
5. She asked me to pick up the kids after school.	**e.** my mother
6. He told me to bring a dictionary tomorrow.	**f.** my wife
7. He asked me not to tell anyone about his new girlfriend.	**g.** my teacher

B **PAIR WORK** Can you think of another request each person might make?

A: A doctor might also tell a patient to get more exercise.
B: . . . or to avoid eating greasy foods.

GRAMMAR FOCUS

Reported speech: requests ▶

Original request	Reported request
Bring a dictionary tomorrow.	He **said to bring** a dictionary tomorrow. He **told me to bring** a dictionary tomorrow.
Don't stay out past midnight.	She **said not to stay** out past midnight. She **told me not to stay** out past midnight.
Can you play your music more quietly?	He **asked me to play** my music more quietly.

A Amanda is having a surprise party for Albert. Look at what she told the guests. Write each request using *say, tell,* or *ask.* Then compare with a partner.

1. Meet at Albert's apartment at 7:30.   *She told them to meet at Albert's apartment at 7:30.*
2. Can you bring your favorite music? ....
3. Don't bring any food. ....
4. Can you bring a small gift for Albert? ....
5. Don't spend more than $10 on the gift. ....
6. Keep the party a secret. ....

B GROUP WORK Imagine you're planning a class party. Write four requests. Then take turns reading your requests and changing them into reported requests.

> Juan: Bring something good to eat to the party!
> Sonia: Juan told us to bring something good to eat.

> Noriko: Can you help me clean up after the party?
> Jin-sook: Noriko asked us to help her clean up.

4 **SPEAKING** *What a request!*

A Think of requests that people have made recently. Write two things people asked you to do and two things people asked you *not* to do.

Person	Request
my mom	get a haircut
....	....
....	....
....	....
....	....

B GROUP WORK Compare with others. Who has the most interesting or unusual requests?

5 WORD POWER *Verb and noun pairs*

A Find words or phrases in the list that are usually paired with each verb. Then compare with a partner.

✓ anger   ✓ your congratulations   a lie
✓ an apology   a criticism   a reason
  a complaint   an excuse   your regrets
✓ a compliment   an invitation   sympathy
  a concern   ✓ a joke   the truth

express	*anger*	....	....
give	*a compliment*	....	....
make	*an apology*	....	....
offer	*your congratulations*	....	....
tell	*a joke*	....	....

B **PAIR WORK** In what situations do you do the things in part A?
Write five sentences about things you *never, sometimes,* or *always* do.
Then take turns reading your sentences and asking questions.

A: I never tell a lie.
B: Are you sure? What if someone invited you to a party, but you didn't want to go?

6 CONVERSATION *Are you doing anything on Saturday?*

A ▶ Listen and practice.

Albert: Hi, Daniel.
Daniel: Oh, hi, Albert. How are things?
Albert: Just fine, thanks. Uh, are you doing anything on Saturday night?
Daniel: Hmm. Saturday night? Let me think. Oh, yes. My cousin just called to say he was flying in that night. I told him I would pick him up.
Albert: Oh, that's too bad! It's my birthday. I'm having dinner with Amanda, and I thought I'd invite more people and make it a party.
Daniel: Gee, I'm really sorry, but I won't be able to make it.
Albert: I'm sorry, too. But that's OK.

B **PAIR WORK** Act out the conversation in part A.
Make up your own excuse for not accepting
Albert's invitation.

7 LISTENING *He said, she said*

A  Listen to Albert inviting friends to his party on Saturday. What excuses do people give for not coming? Match the person to the excuse.

1. Scott ....
2. Fumiko ....
3. Manuel ....
4. Regina ....

    a. She said that she wasn't feeling well.
    b. He said he was taking his mother to a dance club.
    c. She said she had houseguests for the weekend.
    d. He said that he would be out of town.
    e. She said she might go out with friends.
    f. He said he was going away with his family.

B Listen. What happens on the night of Albert's birthday?

8 GRAMMAR FOCUS

Reported speech: statements

Direct statements	Reported statements	
I'**m not feeling** well.	She **said** (that)	she **wasn't feeling** well.
I **have** houseguests for the weekend.		she **had** houseguests for the weekend.
I **made** a tennis date with Kim.		she **had made** a tennis date with Kim.
I **have planned** an exciting trip.		she **had planned** an exciting trip.
We **can't come** tomorrow.	They **told me** (that)	they **couldn't come** tomorrow.
We **will be** out of town.		they **would be** out of town.
We **may go** out with friends.		they **might go** out with friends.

A Sandra is having a party at her house on Saturday. Look at these excuses. Change them into reported speech. Then compare with a partner.

1. Donna: "I have to babysit my nephew that night."
2. William and Brigitte: "We're going out of town for the weekend."
3. Mary: "I've been invited to a wedding on Saturday."
4. James: "I promised to help Dennis move."
5. Anita: "I can't come because I have the flu."
6. Mark: "I'll be studying for a test all weekend."
7. Eva and Randall: "We have to pick someone up at the airport that evening."
8. David: "I may have to work late on Saturday night."

> Donna said she had to babysit her nephew that night. OR
> Donna told her she had to babysit her nephew that night.

B GROUP WORK Imagine you don't want to go to Sandra's party. Take turns making excuses and changing them into reported speech.

A: I'm sorry I can't go. I have tickets to a concert that night.
B: Lucky guy! He said he had tickets to a concert that night.

9 PRONUNCIATION *Reduction of* had *and* would

A ▶ Listen and practice. Notice how **had** and **would** are reduced in the following sentences.

She said she**'d made** the bed. (She said she **had made** the bed.)
She said she**'d make** the bed. (She said she **would make** the bed.)

B ▶ Listen to four sentences. Check (✓) the reduced form that you hear.

1. ☐ had   2. ☐ had   3. ☐ had   4. ☐ had
   ☐ would   ☐ would   ☐ would   ☐ would

10 WRITING *A report*

A Interview your classmates and take notes. Use your notes to write a report describing what people told you. Use reported speech.

	Name	Response
What did you do last weekend?	....	....
What new TV show have you seen recently?	....	....
Where are you going after class?	....	....
What are your plans this evening?	....	....
What will you do this weekend?	....	....

B GROUP WORK Read your report, but don't give names. Others guess the person.

"Someone told me that she'd watched three movies last weekend."

11 SPEAKING *Good intentions*

A GROUP WORK What are some things you would like to do in the future? Think of three intentions.

A: I'm going to learn how to sail.
B: That sounds fun. Are you going to take lessons?

B CLASS ACTIVITY Report the best intentions you heard. Then predict which ones will happen.

"Tatyana said she was going to learn how to sail, but she didn't want to take lessons."

12 INTERCHANGE 16 *Excuses, excuses*

Make some plans. Student A, go to Interchange 16A on page 129; Student B, go to Interchange 16B on page 131.

The Truth About Lying

Is it ever better to tell a lie than the truth? If so, when?

Most of us are taught to believe that lying is wrong. But it seems that everybody tells lies – not big lies, but what we call "white lies." If we believe that lying is wrong, why do we do it? Most of the time, people have very good reasons for lying. For example, they might want to protect a friendship or someone's feelings. So, when do we lie and who do we lie to? A recent study found that the average person lies about seven times a day. Here are some reasons why.

1 **Lying to hide something:** People often lie because they want to hide something from someone. For example, a son doesn't tell his parents that he's dating a girl because he doesn't think they will like her. Instead, he says he's going out with the guys.

2 **Lying to make an excuse:** Sometimes people lie because they don't want to do something. For example, someone invites you to a party. You think it will be boring, so you say you're busy.

3 **Lying to avoid sharing bad news:** Sometimes we don't want to tell someone bad news. For example, you have just had a very bad day at work, but you don't feel like talking about it. So if someone asks you about your day, you just say that everything was fine.

4 **Lying to make someone feel good:** Often we stretch the truth to make someone feel good. For example, your friend cooks dinner for you, but it tastes terrible. Do you say so? No. You probably say, "Mmm, this is delicious!"

A Read the article. Then complete the summary with information from the article.

It isn't necessarily .... to lie. It's probably OK to lie if you want to protect ....
or .... The main reasons for lying are to .... ,
to .... , to .... , or to ....

B Look at these situations. For each example, write the number of the appropriate reason.

.... 1. Your friend gives you an ugly shirt for your birthday. You say, "Oh, it's great!"
.... 2. Someone you don't like invites you to a movie, so you say, "I've already seen it."
.... 3. You lost your job and are having trouble finding a new one. When an old friend calls to find out how you are, you say you're doing well.
.... 4. You're planning a surprise party for a friend. To get him to come over at the right time, you ask him to stop by to see your new motorcycle.

C **GROUP WORK** Can you think of other reasons people tell white lies? What white lies have you told recently?

Units 15–16 Progress check

SELF-ASSESSMENT

How well can you do these things? Check (✓) the boxes.

I can	Very well	OK	A little
Speculate about imaginary events (Ex. 1)	☐	☐	☐
Ask for and give advice and suggestions about past events (Ex. 2)	☐	☐	☐
Understand and report requests (Ex. 3)	☐	☐	☐
Report what people say (Ex. 4)	☐	☐	☐

1 DISCUSSION *Interesting situations*

A What would you do in these situations? Complete the statements.

If I found a valuable piece of jewelry in the park, ...
If a friend gave me a present I didn't like, ...
If I wasn't invited to a party I wanted to attend, ...
If a classmate wanted to copy my homework, ...
If someone took my clothes while I was swimming, ...

B GROUP WORK Compare your responses. For each situation, choose one to tell the class.

A: What would you do if you found some jewelry in the park?
B: I'd probably keep it. You'd never be able to find the owner.

2 SPEAKING *Dilemmas*

A Make up two situations like the one below. Think about experiences
you have had or heard about at work, home, or school.

"A friend visited me recently. We had a great time at first, but
she became annoying. She borrowed my clothes and refused to
pay for things. After two weeks, I told her she had to leave
because my parents were coming."

B PAIR WORK Take turns sharing your situations.
Ask for advice and suggestions.

A: What would you have done?
B: Well, I would have told her to leave after three days.

3 LISTENING *Take a message.*

A Listen to the conversations. Who would make these requests?
Match conversations 1 to 6 to the correct person.

.... a. boss   .... c. neighbor   .... e. classmate
.... b. doctor   .... d. parent   .... f. teacher

B ▶ Listen again. Complete the requests.

1. Please ....   4. Can .... ?
2. Can .... ?   5. Please ....
3. Don't ....   6. Please don't ....

C **PAIR WORK** Work with a partner. Imagine these requests were for you.
Take turns reporting the requests to your partner.

4 GAME *Tell the truth.*

A Think of situations when you expressed anger, gave an excuse, or
made a complaint. Write a brief statement about each situation.

> I once complained about the food in a restaurant.

B **CLASS ACTIVITY** Play a game. Choose three students to be contestants.

Step 1: The contestants compare their statements and choose one. This statement should be true
about only one student. The other two students should pretend they had the experience.

Step 2: The contestants stand in front of the class. Each contestant reads the same statement. The rest
of the class must ask questions to find out who isn't telling the truth.

> Contestant A, what restaurant were you in?

> Contestant B, what was wrong with the food?

> Contestant C, what did the waiter do?

Step 3: Who isn't telling the truth? What did he or she say to make you think that?

"I don't think Contestant A is telling the truth. He said he couldn't
remember the name of the restaurant!"

WHAT'S NEXT?

Look at your Self-assessment again. Do you need to review anything?

Interchange activities

A **CLASS ACTIVITY** Go around the class and find out the information below. Then ask follow-up questions and take notes. Write a classmate's name only once.

Find someone who	Name	Notes
1. used to look very different **"Did you use to look very different?"**		
2. always listened to his or her teachers **"Did you always listen to your teachers?"**		
3. had a pet when he or she was little **"Did you have a pet when you were little?"**		
4. wanted to be a movie star **"Did you ever want to be a movie star?"**		
5. changed schools when he or she was a child **" .... ?"**		
6. used to argue with his or her brothers and sisters **" .... ?"**		
7. got in trouble a lot as a child **" .... ?"**		
8. used to have a favorite toy **" .... ?"**		

B **GROUP WORK** Tell the group the most interesting thing you learned about your classmates.

A PAIR WORK Look at the photos and slogans below. What do you think the theme of each tourism campaign is?

possible themes		
art	food	nature
culture	history	shopping
entertainment	music	sports

Rio de Janeiro
"Carnaval and Natural Marvels"

Cairo
"The Earth's Mother"

Hong Kong
"A Diner's Paradise"

Salzburg
"A Musical Banquet"

B GROUP WORK Imagine you are planning a campaign to attract more tourists to one of the cities above or to a city of your choice. Use the ideas below or your own ideas to discuss the campaign.

a good time to visit
famous historical attractions
special events or festivals
nice areas to stay
interesting places to see
memorable things to do

A: Do you know when a good time to visit Rio is?
B: I think February or March is a good time because . . .

C GROUP WORK What will be the theme of your campaign? What slogan will you use?

A Complete this questionnaire with information about yourself.

☆My Wish List☆

1. What kind of vacation do you wish you could take?
   I wish I could

2. What sport do you wish you could play?

3. Which country do you wish you could live in?

4. What kind of home do you wish you could have?

5. What kind of pet do you wish you could have?

6. What languages do you wish you could speak?

7. Which musical instruments do you wish you could play?

8. What kind of car do you wish you could buy?

9. What famous people do you wish you could meet?

10. What do you wish you could do right now?

B **PAIR WORK** Compare your questionnaires. Take turns asking and answering questions about your wishes.

A: What kind of vacation do you wish you could take?
B: I wish I could go on a safari.
A: Really? Why?
B: Well, I could take some great pictures of wild animals!

C **CLASS ACTIVITY** Imagine you are at a class reunion. It is ten years since you completed the questionnaire in part A. Tell the class about some wishes that have come true for your partner.

"Sue is a photographer now. She travels to Africa every year and takes pictures of wild animals. Her photos are in many magazines."

A How much do you really know about your classmates? Look at the survey and add two more situations to items 1 and 2.

	Name	Notes
1. Find someone who has . . .		
a. forgotten a password		
b. lost his or her phone		
c. been on TV		
d. cried during a movie		
e. sung in public		
f.		
g.		
2. Find someone who has never . . .		
a. driven a car		
b. used a recipe to cook		
c. played a video game		
d. baked cookies		
e. been camping		
f.		
g.		

B CLASS ACTIVITY Go around the class and ask the questions. Write the names of classmates who answer "yes" for item 1 and "no" for item 2. Then ask follow-up questions and take notes.

A: Have you ever forgotten a password?
B: Yes, I have.
A: Did you ever remember it?
B: Yes, but it took an hour!

A: Have you ever driven a car?
C: No, I haven't.
A: Why not?
C: Because I don't have a driver's license.

C GROUP WORK Compare the information in your surveys.

Student A

A PAIR WORK You and your partner are going to take a trip. You have a brochure for a biking trip, and your partner has a brochure for a surfing trip.

First, find out about the surfing trip. Ask your partner questions about these things.

the length of the trip   the cost of the trip   what the price includes
the accommodations   entertainment options   nighttime activities

B PAIR WORK Now use the information in this brochure to answer your partner's questions about the biking trip.

Colorado Biking Trip
14-day biking, camping, and hiking tour

Visit these beautiful sites in the Rocky Mountains:
◆ Estes Park
◆ The Continental Divide
◆ Peaceful Valley Lodge
◆ Gem Lake

Accommodations:
Deluxe campsites with hot showers

Price includes:
All meals, daily bicycle and equipment rental, bike safety class

Nighttime activities:
Campfire sing-alongs, stargazing, stories from the Old West

Additional activities:
◆ Hike in Rocky Mountain National Park
◆ Spot wildlife, such as elk, moose, and eagles
◆ Visit an old ghost town

Tour cost:
$1,699

C PAIR WORK Decide which trip you are going to take. Then explain your choice to the class.

A PAIR WORK Look at these situations and act out conversations. Apologize and then give an excuse, admit a mistake, or make an offer or a promise.

useful expressions

I'm sorry. / I didn't realize. / I forgot.
You're right. / I was wrong.
I'll . . . right away.
I'll make sure to . . . / I promise I'll . . .

Student A: You're the customer.

Student B: You're the hairstylist.

A: My hair! You ruined my hair!
B: ....

Student A: You own the backpack.

Student B: You own the puppy.

A: Hey! Your puppy has my bag!
B: ....

Student A: You're driving the red car.

Student B: You're driving the blue car.

A: Watch where you're going!
B: ....

Student A: You're the customer.

Student B: You're the cashier.

A: Oh, dear. I don't seem to have any cash. . . .
B: ....

B GROUP WORK Have you ever experienced situations like these?
What happened? What did you do? Share your stories.

Student B

A **PAIR WORK** You and your partner are going to take a trip. You have a brochure for a surfing trip, and your partner has a brochure for a biking trip.

First, use the information in this brochure to answer your partner's questions about the surfing trip.

CALIFORNIA

SURFING!

15-day tour for beach lovers

Accommodations:
• Single rooms in beachfront hotels

Price includes:
• All meals
• Daily surfboard rental
• 3-hour surfing class

Nighttime activities:
• Beach barbecue
• Club dancing
• Moonlight cruise

Additional activities:
• Visit Universal Studios and Disneyland
• Tour Beverly Hills and see movie stars' homes

Tour cost:
• $1,999

Visit these beautiful Southern California beaches

El Capitán in Santa Barbara

Surfrider in Malibu

The Wedge at Newport Beach

Doheny at Dana Point

B **PAIR WORK** Now find out about the biking trip. Ask your partner questions about these things.

the length of the trip	the cost of the trip	what the price includes
the accommodations	entertainment options	nighttime activities

C **PAIR WORK** Decide which trip you are going to take. Then explain your choice to the class.

A GROUP WORK Look at the four problems that people called a radio program about. What advice would you give each caller? Discuss possible suggestions and then choose the best one.

Caller 1: My family and I are going away on vacation. How can we make sure our home is safe from burglars while we're gone?

Caller 2: A classmate wants to borrow my MP3 player to take with him on vacation. I don't want to lend it to him. What can I say?

Caller 3: I'm going to meet my girlfriend's parents tomorrow for the first time. How can I make a good impression?

Caller 4: I'm really into social networking, but in the past week, five people I hardly know have asked me to be their friend.

B PAIR WORK Take turns "calling" a radio station and explaining your problems. Use the situations above or create new ones. Your partner should give you advice.

A: My family and I are going away on vacation. How can we make sure our home is safe from burglars while we're gone?

B: Well, don't forget to lock all the windows. Oh, and make sure to . . .

SPECIAL OCCASIONS

A CLASS ACTIVITY How do your classmates celebrate special occasions? Go around the class and ask the questions below. If someone answers "yes," write down his or her name. Ask for more information and take notes.

QUESTION	NAME	NOTES
1. Does your family have big get-togethers?		
2. Have you bought flowers for someone special recently?		
3. Do you like to watch street parades?		
4. Do you ever wear traditional clothes?		
5. Has someone given you money recently as a gift?		
6. Have you ever given someone a surprise birthday party?		
7. Will you celebrate your next birthday with a party?		
8. Did you get any cards on your last birthday?		
9. Do you ever give friends birthday presents?		
10. Is New Year's your favorite time of the year?		
11. Do you ever celebrate a holiday with fireworks?		

A: Does your family have big get-togethers?
B: Yes, we do.
A: What do you do when you get together?
B: Well, we have a big meal. After we eat, we play games and watch old home movies.

B PAIR WORK Compare your information with a partner.

CONSIDER THE CONSEQUENCES

A Read over this questionnaire. Check (✓) the box for your opinion.

1 If people watch less TV, they'll talk more with their families.
- ☐ I agree.
- ☐ I don't agree.
- ☐ It depends.

2 If children watch a lot of violent programs on TV, they'll become violent themselves.
- ☐ I agree.
- ☐ I don't agree.
- ☐ It depends.

3 If people work only four days a week, their lives will improve.
- ☐ I agree.
- ☐ I don't agree.
- ☐ It depends.

4 If a child has brothers and sisters, he or she won't ever feel lonely or sad.
- ☐ I agree.
- ☐ I don't agree.
- ☐ It depends.

5 If a woman works outside the home, her children won't be happy.
- ☐ I agree.
- ☐ I don't agree.
- ☐ It depends.

6 If you have too many online friends, you'll have fewer "real" friends.
- ☐ I agree.
- ☐ I don't agree.
- ☐ It depends.

7 If the city lowers the cost of public transportation, more people will use it.
- ☐ I agree.
- ☐ I don't agree.
- ☐ It depends.

8 If there is a heavy fine for littering, our streets will be much cleaner.
- ☐ I agree.
- ☐ I don't agree.
- ☐ It depends.

9 If teachers put their class assignments on the Internet, students might see homework as a fun activity and enjoy doing it.
- ☐ I agree.
- ☐ I don't agree.
- ☐ It depends.

10 If teachers give harder tests, students will study harder for them.
- ☐ I agree.
- ☐ I don't agree.
- ☐ It depends.

B GROUP WORK Compare your opinions. Be prepared to give reasons for your opinions.

A: I think if people watch less TV, they'll talk more with their families.
B: I don't really agree.
C: Why not?
B: If they don't watch TV, they'll do something else.
They may spend all day on the computer.

A Look at the following job descriptions. Choose one job that you'd like to apply for.

JOB BOARD

Find a job . . . |

Post a job . . . |

Marketing Manager

Requirements:
• A business degree or marketing experience
• Able to travel and work long hours
• Enjoy sports and fitness activities

Responsibilities:
• Interviewing people about their sports preferences, writing reports, and working with famous athletes

Personal Assistant

Requirements:
• Excellent telephone skills
• Able to work flexible hours
• Able to take orders and make important decisions

Responsibilities:
• Maintaining the calendar of a busy celebrity, scheduling meetings, and preparing the star for public appearances

Activities Director

Requirements:
• Experience working with tourists
• A "people person"
• Outgoing and creative personality

Responsibilities:
• Organizing all leisure activities on a popular cruise ship, including planning daily tours, special menus, and nightly entertainment

JOB FAIR

B PAIR WORK Take turns interviewing each other for the job you each want. Give as much information as you can to show that you are the right person for the job.

C PAIR WORK Would you hire your partner for the job? Why or why not?

D PAIR WORK What is your dream job?

useful questions

What kind of degree do you have?
What work experience do you have?
What hours can you work?
Do you mind working . . . ?
Are you interested in working with . . . ?
Why should I hire you for the job?

WHO IS THIS BY?

A List one movie, one TV show, one song, and one book.

B GROUP WORK Take turns making a statement about each item. Does everyone agree with each statement?

A: *The Hobbit* was filmed in the United States.
B: Are you sure? Wasn't it filmed in Australia?
C: I'm pretty sure it was New Zealand.

C Now think of other famous creations and creators. Complete the chart. Make some of the items true and some of them false.

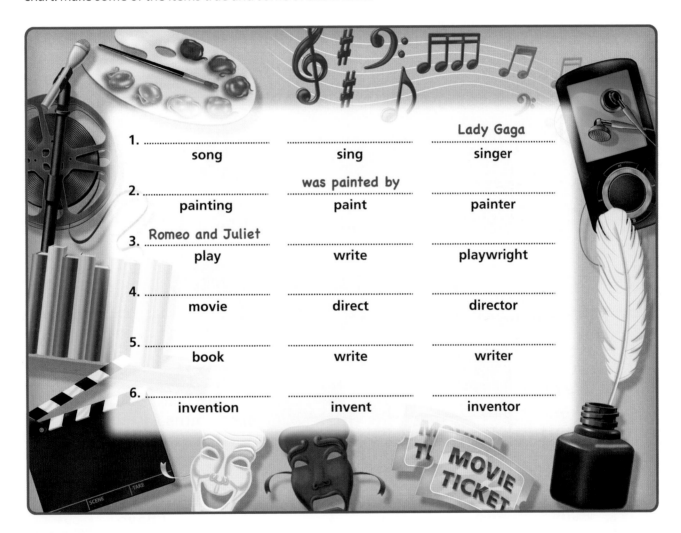

					Lady Gaga
1.	song		sing		singer
2.	painting	was painted by	paint		painter
3.	Romeo and Juliet play		write		playwright
4.	movie		direct		director
5.	book		write		writer
6.	invention		invent		inventor

D GROUP WORK Make a statement about each item to your group members. Ask them to decide which statements are true and which are false.

A: The song "Bad Romance" was sung by Lady Gaga.
B: I think that's false.
C: No, that's true. I'm sure of it.

A GROUP WORK Play the board game. Follow these instructions.

1. Use small pieces of paper with your initials on them as markers.

2. Take turns by tossing a coin:

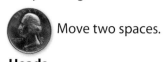 Move two spaces.

Heads

 Move one space.

Tails

3. Complete the sentence in the space you land on. Others ask two follow-up questions to get more information.

A: When I was little, I had a red bicycle.
B: Oh, really? Did you ride it every day?
A: No, I never rode it.
C: Why didn't you ever ride it?

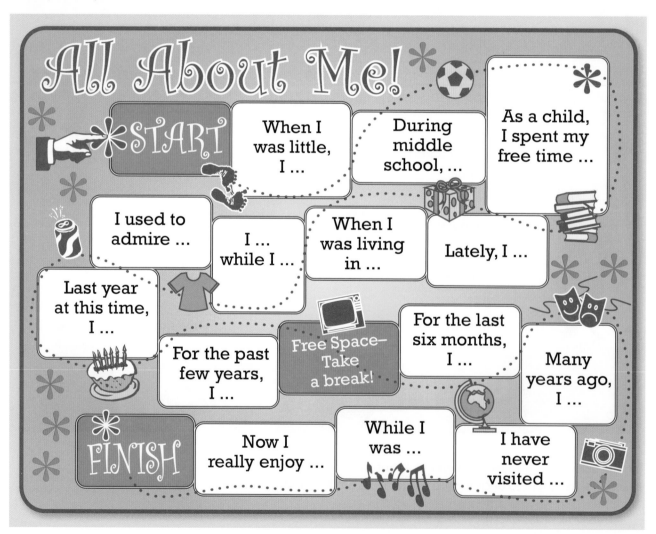

B CLASS ACTIVITY Tell the class an interesting fact that you learned about someone in your group.

"On his first day of middle school, Danny lost his backpack."

A Complete this questionnaire.

What is the name of a TV or movie star . . . ?
1. that reminds you of someone in your family
   _____
2. that has beautiful eyes
   _____
3. who does things to help society
   _____
4. who has a beautiful speaking voice
   _____
5. who isn't good-looking but who is very talented
   _____

What is the name of a TV show or movie . . . ?
6. that made you feel sad
   _____
7. that made you laugh a lot
   _____
8. which scared you
   _____
9. which had great music
   _____
10. that was about a ridiculous story
    _____

B **PAIR WORK** Compare your questionnaires. Ask follow-up questions of your own.

A: What is the name of a TV or movie star that reminds you of someone in your family?
B: Tom Cruise.
A: Who does he remind you of?
B: My brother, Todd.
A: Really? Why?
B: Because he looks like my brother. They have the same smile.

A PAIR WORK Look at this scene of a crowded restaurant. What do you think is happening in each of the five situations? Look at people's body language for clues.

A: Why do you think the woman in situation 2 looks upset?
B: Well, she might be having a fight with . . .

A: What do you think the man's gesture in situation 2 means?
B: Maybe it means he . . .

B GROUP WORK Compare your interpretations. Do you agree or disagree?

Student A

A PAIR WORK You and your partner want to get together. Ask and answer questions to find a day when you are both free. You also want to keep time open for other friends, so make up excuses for those days. Write your partner's excuses on the calendar.

A: Do you want to go out on the 2nd?
B: I'm sorry. I'm going to my friend's wedding. Are you free on the 1st?
A: Well, I . . .

B PAIR WORK Now work with another Student A. Discuss the excuses Student B gave you. Decide which excuses were probably true and which ones were probably not true.

A: Anna said that on the 9th she had to stay home and reorganize her clothes closet. That was probably not true.
B: I agree. I think . . .

A What would you do in each of these situations? Circle **a**, **b**, or **c**. If you think you would do something else, write your suggestion next to **d**.

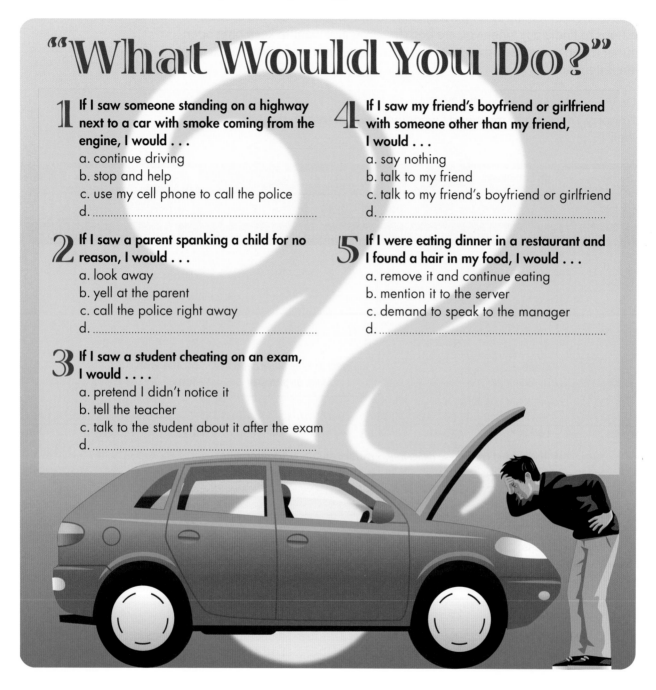

"What Would You Do?"

1 If I saw someone standing on a highway next to a car with smoke coming from the engine, I would . . .
  a. continue driving
  b. stop and help
  c. use my cell phone to call the police
  d. ....

2 If I saw a parent spanking a child for no reason, I would . . .
  a. look away
  b. yell at the parent
  c. call the police right away
  d. ....

3 If I saw a student cheating on an exam, I would . . . .
  a. pretend I didn't notice it
  b. tell the teacher
  c. talk to the student about it after the exam
  d. ....

4 If I saw my friend's boyfriend or girlfriend with someone other than my friend, I would . . .
  a. say nothing
  b. talk to my friend
  c. talk to my friend's boyfriend or girlfriend
  d. ....

5 If I were eating dinner in a restaurant and I found a hair in my food, I would . . .
  a. remove it and continue eating
  b. mention it to the server
  c. demand to speak to the manager
  d. ....

B GROUP WORK Compare your choices for each situation in part A.

A: What would you do if you saw someone standing on a highway next to a car with smoke coming from the engine?
B: Honestly, I would probably continue driving.
C: Really? I wouldn't. I would . . .

C CLASS ACTIVITY Take a class survey. Find out which choice was most popular for each situation. Talk about any other suggestions people added for **d**.

Student B

A PAIR WORK You and your partner want to get together. Ask and answer questions to find a day when you are both free. You also want to keep time open for other friends, so make up excuses for those days. Write your partner's excuses on the calendar.

A: Do you want to go out on the 2nd?
B: I'm sorry. I'm going to my friend's wedding. Are you free on the 1st?
A: Well, I . . .

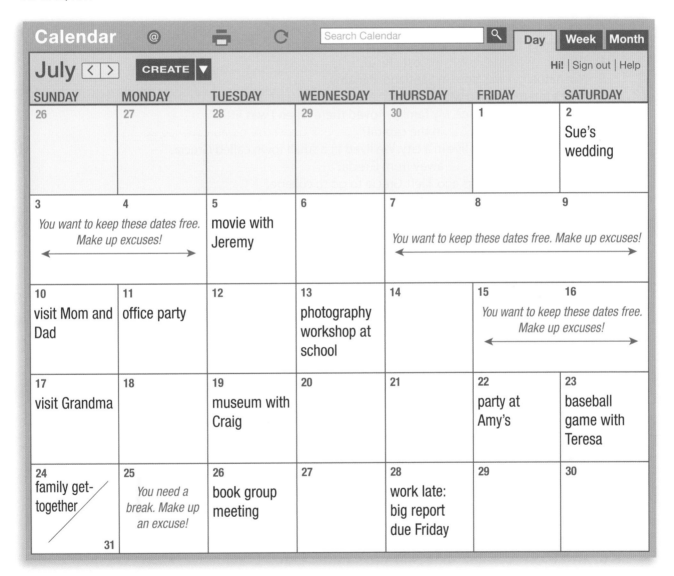

| Calendar | | | | | Search Calendar | Day | Week | Month |

July < > CREATE ▼

Hi! | Sign out | Help

SUNDAY	MONDAY	TUESDAY	WEDNESDAY	THURSDAY	FRIDAY	SATURDAY
26	27	28	29	30	1	2 Sue's wedding
3 *You want to keep these dates free. Make up excuses!* ◄─────►	4	5 movie with Jeremy	6	7 *You want to keep these dates free. Make up excuses!* ◄─────────►	8	9
10 visit Mom and Dad	11 office party	12	13 photography workshop at school	14	15 *You want to keep these dates free. Make up excuses!* ◄───►	16
17 visit Grandma	18	19 museum with Craig	20	21	22 party at Amy's	23 baseball game with Teresa
24 family get-together / 31	25 *You need a break. Make up an excuse!*	26 book group meeting	27	28 work late: big report due Friday	29	30

B PAIR WORK Now work with another Student B. Discuss the excuses Student A gave you. Decide which excuses were probably true and which ones were probably not true.

A: Joe said that on the 6th he had to stay home and reorganize his clothes closet. That was probably not true.
B: I agree. I think . . .

Grammar plus

Unit 1

1 Past tense (page 3)

▶ Use a form of *be* with *born*: I **was born** here. (NOT: I ~~born~~ here.) Don't use a form of *be* with the verb *die*: He **died** last year. (NOT: He ~~was died~~ last year.)

Complete the conversation.

1. A: Do you live around here?
   B: No, I don't. I'm from Costa Rica.
   A: Really? <u>Were you born</u> in Costa Rica?
   B: No. Actually, I was born in Santiago, Panama.
2. A: That's interesting. So where .... ?
   B: I grew up in Costa Rica. My family moved there when I was little.
3. A: .... in the capital?
   B: No, my family didn't live in a city. We lived in a small town called Grecia.
4. A: .... away from Grecia?
   B: Oh, about eight years ago. I left Grecia to go to college.
5. A: Where .... to college?
   B: I went to college in San Jose, and I live there now.
6. A: And .... to Miami?
   B: I got here a few days ago. I'm visiting my cousin.

2 *Used to* (page 5)

▶ Use the base form of *used to* in questions and negative statements: Did you **use to** play sports? (NOT: Did you ~~used to~~ play sports?) I didn't **use to** like bananas. (NOT: I didn't ~~used to~~ like bananas.)
▶ Don't use *never* in negative statements: I **never used to** wear sunglasses. (NOT: I never ~~didn't use to~~ wear sunglasses.)

Complete the conversations with the correct form of *used to*.

1. A: Hey, Dad. What kinds of clothes <u>did you use to</u> wear – you know, when you were a kid?
   B: Oh, we .... wear jeans and T-shirts – like you kids do now.
   A: Really? .... Mom .... dress like that, too?
   B: No, not really. She never .... like wearing pants. She always .... wear skirts and dresses.
2. A: .... you .... play a sport when you were a kid?
   B: Well, I .... be a swimmer. My sister and I .... swim on a team.
   A: Wow, that's cool! Were you good?
   B: Yeah. I .... win gold medals all the time. And my sister .... be the fastest swimmer on the team.

Unit 2

1 Expressions of quantity (page 9)

> ▶ Count nouns have a plural form that usually ends in -s. Noncount nouns don't have a plural form because you can't separate and count them: Are there any **parking garages** around here? BUT Is there any **parking** around here? (NOT: Are there any parkings around here?)

Complete the conversations with the correct words in parentheses.

1. A: There's .... (too many / too much) traffic in this city. There should be .... (fewer / less) cars downtown.
   B: The problem is there .... (aren't / isn't) enough public transportation.
   A: You're right. We should have more .... (bus / buses). There .... (aren't / isn't) enough of them during rush hour.
2. A: How do you like your new neighborhood?
   B: It's terrible, actually. There's .... (too many / too much) noise and .... (too few / too little) parking.
   A: That's too bad. There .... (aren't / isn't) enough parking spaces in my neighborhood either.
3. A: Did you hear about the changes to the city center? Starting next month, there will be more bicycle .... (lane / lanes) and .... (fewer / less) street parking.
   B: That's good. There .... (are too many / is too much) pollution downtown. I'm sure there will be .... (fewer / less) accidents, too.
   A: That's true.

2 Indirect questions from Wh-questions (page 11)

> ▶ Indirect questions are often polite requests for information. *Can you tell me how much this magazine costs?* sounds more polite than *How much does this magazine cost?*

Complete the conversation with indirect questions.

1. A: Excuse me. Can you <u>tell me where the post office is</u> ....?
   B: Yes, of course. The post office is on the next corner.
2. A: And could you ....?
   B: You can find a really good restaurant on Central Avenue.
3. A: OK. Do you ....?
   B: Yes. The restaurant is called Giorgio's.
4. A: Thanks. Can you ....?
   B: Yes. They serve Italian food.
5. A: Oh, good! Do you ....?
   B: It opens at 5:00. Tell them Joe sent you!
   A: OK, Joe. Thanks for everything! Bye now.

Unit 3

1 Evaluations and comparisons (page 17)

▶ In evaluations, *enough* goes after adjectives and before nouns.
adjective + *enough*: This house isn't **bright enough**. (NOT: This house isn't ~~enough bright~~.)
noun + *enough*: This house doesn't have **enough light**. (NOT: This house doesn't have ~~light enough~~.)

A Read each situation. Then write two sentences describing the problem, one sentence with *not . . . enough* and one with *too*.

1. Our family needs a big house. This house is very small.
   a. This house isn't big enough for us.
   b. This house is too small for us.
2. We want to live on a quiet street. This street is very noisy.
   a. ....
   b. ....
3. We need three bedrooms. This house has only two.
   a. ....
   b. ....
4. We want a spacious living room. This one is cramped.
   a. ....
   b. ....

B Rewrite the comparisons using *as . . . as*. Use *just* when possible.

1. My new apartment is smaller than my old one.
   My new apartment isn't as large as my old one.
2. This neighborhood is safer than my old one.
   ....
3. This apartment has a lot of privacy. My old one did, too.
   ....
4. My rent is reasonable now. It was very high before.
   ....

2 *Wish* (page 20)

▶ Use *could* (the past of *can*) and *would* (the past of *will*) with *wish*: I **can't** move right now, but I wish I **could**. My landlord **won't** paint my apartment, but I wish he **would**.

Match the problems with the wishes.

1. My house isn't very nice. ....c....
2. It costs a lot to live here. ....
3. My landlord won't call me back. ....
4. I have noisy neighbors. ....
5. I don't like living alone. ....
6. The buses don't run very often. ....

a. I wish I could find a good roommate.
b. I wish he'd return my calls.
c. I wish it were more attractive.
d. I wish I could afford a car.
e. I wish their music weren't so loud.
f. I wish it weren't so expensive.

Unit 4

1 Simple past vs. present perfect (page 23)

> ▶ Use the simple past – not the present perfect – when you say when an event ended:
> I **had** sushi <u>last night</u>. (NOT: I've had sushi last night.)

Complete the conversations. Choose the best forms.

1. A: What .... (did you have / have you had) for dinner
   last night?
   B: I .... (tried / have tried) Indian food for the first time.
   .... (Did you ever have / Have you ever had) it?
   A: A friend and I .... (ate / have eaten) at an Indian
   restaurant just last week. It .... (was / has been)
   delicious!

2. A: .... (Did you ever take / Have you ever taken) a
   cooking class?
   B: No, I .... (didn't / haven't). How about you?
   A: I .... (took / have taken) a few classes. My last
   class .... (was / has been) in December. We
   .... (learned / have learned) how to make some
   wonderful Spanish dishes.

3. A: I .... (watched / have watched) a great cooking
   show on TV yesterday.
   B: Really? I .... (never saw / have never seen) a
   cooking show. .... (Was it / Has it been) boring?
   A: No, it .... (wasn't / hasn't). It ....
   (was / has been) very interesting!

2 Sequence adverbs (page 25)

> ▶ *Then, next,* and *after that* mean the same. *First* comes first, and *finally* comes last; you
> can use the other adverbs in any order: **First,** put some water in a pan. **Then/Next,/
> After that,** put the eggs in the water. **Finally,** boil the eggs for seven minutes.

Unscramble the steps in this recipe for hamburgers. Then write the steps in order.

| salt and pepper | add | in the bowl | to the meat | then |

.... : ....

| two pounds of chopped beef | put | in a bowl | first, |

..Step 1.. : First, put two pounds of chopped beef in a bowl.

| put | the burgers | in a pan | finally, | and cook for 10 minutes |

.... : ....

| next, | the meat | and the salt and pepper | mix | together |

.... : ....

| into four burgers | after that, | with your hands | form the meat |

.... : ....

Unit 5

1 Future with *be going to* and *will* (page 31)

> ▶ Use the base form of the verb – not the infinitive (*to* + base form) – with *will*: I think I'**ll go** to Hawaii next winter. (NOT: I think I'll ~~to~~ go to Hawaii next winter.)
>
> ▶ Use *be going to* – not *will* – when you know something is going to happen: Look at those black clouds. It'**s going to** rain. (NOT: It ~~will~~ rain.)

Complete the conversation with the correct form of *be going to* or *will* and the verbs in parentheses.

A: It's Friday – at last! What ...*are you going to do*.. (do) this weekend?
B: I'm not sure. I'm really tired, so I probably .... (not do) anything exciting. Maybe I .... (see) a movie on Saturday. How about you? How .... (spend) your weekend?
A: My wife and I .... (do) some work on our house. We .... (paint) the living room on Saturday. On Sunday, we .... (clean) all the rugs.
B: .... (do) anything fun?
A: Oh, I think we .... (have) a lot of fun. We like working around the house. And Sunday's my birthday, so we .... (have) dinner at my favorite Italian restaurant.
B: Now that sounds like fun!

2 Modals for necessity and suggestion (page 33)

> ▶ Some modals for necessity and suggestion are stronger than others.
> Weak (for advice or an opinion): *should, ought to*
> Stronger (for a warning): *had better*
> Strongest (for an obligation): *must, need to, have to*

Choose the correct word or words to complete the advice to travelers.

1. You .... (must / should) show identification at the airport. They won't allow you on a plane without an official ID.
2. Your ID .... (needs to / ought to) have a picture of you on it. It's required.
3. The picture of you .... (has to / ought to) be recent. They won't accept an old photo.
4. Travelers .... (must / should) get to the airport at least two hours before their flight. It's not a good idea to get there later than that.
5. All travelers .... (have to / had better) go through airport security. It's necessary for passenger safety.
6. Many airlines don't serve food, so passengers on long flights probably .... (must / ought to) buy something to eat at the airport.

Unit 6

1 Two-part verbs; *will* for responding to requests (page 37)

> ▶ Two-part verbs are verb + particle.
> ▶ If the object of a two-part verb is a noun, the noun can come before or after the particle: **Take out** the trash./**Take** the trash **out**.
> ▶ If the object is a pronoun, the pronoun must come before the particle: **Take** it **out**. (NOT: Take ~~out it~~.)

Write conversations. First, rewrite the request given by changing the position of the particle. Then write a response to the request using *it* or *them*.

1. Put away your clothes, please.
   A: Put your clothes away, please.
   B: OK. I'll put them away.
2. Turn the lights on, please.
   A: ....
   B: ....
3. Please turn your music down.
   A: ....
   B: ....
4. Clean up the kitchen, please.
   A: ....
   B: ....
5. Turn off your phone, please.
   A: ....
   B: ....

2 Requests with modals and *Would you mind . . . ?* (page 39)

> ▶ Use the base form of the verb – not the infinitive (*to* + base form) – with the modals *can, could,* and *would*: **Could** you **get** me a sandwich? (NOT: Could you ~~to~~ get me a sandwich?)
> ▶ Requests with modals and *Would you mind . . . ?* are polite – even without *please. Can you get me a sandwich?* sounds much more polite than *Get me a sandwich.*

Change these sentences to polite requests. Use the words in parentheses.

1. Bring in the mail. (could)
   Could you bring in the mail?
2. Put your shoes by the door. (would you mind)
   ....
3. Don't leave dishes in the sink. (would you mind)
   ....
4. Change the TV channel. (can)
   ....
5. Don't play ball inside. (would you mind)
   ....
6. Clean up your mess. (would you mind)
   ....
7. Put away the clean towels. (can)
   ....
8. Pick up your things. (could)
   ....

Unit 7

1 Infinitives and gerunds for uses and purposes (page 45)

> ▶ Sentences with infinitives and gerunds mean the same: *I use my cell phone to send text messages* means the same as *I use my cell phone for sending text messages*. Use a gerund – not an infinitive – after *for*: Satellites are used **for studying** weather. (NOT: Satellites are used for ~~to study~~ weather.)

Read each sentence about a technology item. Write two sentences about the item's use and purpose. Use the information in parentheses.

1. My sister's car has a built-in GPS system. (She use / get directions)
   a. *She uses the GPS system to get directions.*
   b. *She uses the GPS system for getting directions.*
2. I love my new smartphone. (I use / take pictures)
   a. ....
   b. ....
3. That's a flash drive. (You use / back up files)
   a. ....
   b. ....
4. My little brother wants his own laptop. (would only use / watch movies and play games)
   a. ....
   b. ....
5. I'm often on my computer all day long. (I use / shop online and do research)
   a. ....
   b. ....

2 Imperatives and infinitives for giving suggestions (page 47)

> ▶ With imperatives and infinitives, *not* goes before – not after – *to*: Try **not to** talk too long. (NOT: Try ~~to not~~ talk too long.)

Rewrite the sentences as suggestions. Use the words in parentheses.

1. When you go to the movies, turn off your phone. (don't forget)
   When you go to the movies, don't forget to turn off your phone.
2. Don't talk on the phone when you're in an elevator. (try)
   ....
3. Don't eat or drink anything when you're at the computer. (be sure)
   ....
4. Clean your computer screen and keyboard once a week. (remember)
   ....
5. Don't use your tablet outside when it's raining. (make sure)
   ....
6. When the bell rings to start class, put your music player away! (be sure)
   ....

Unit 8

1 Relative clauses of time (page 51)

> ▶ Relative clauses with *when* describe the word *time* or a noun that refers to a period of time, such as *day, night, month,* and *year.*

Combine the two sentences using *when.*

1. Thanksgiving is a holiday. Entire families get together.
   Thanksgiving is a holiday when entire families get together.
2. It's a wonderful time. People give thanks for the good things in their lives.

3. It's a day. Everyone eats much more than usual.

4. I remember one particular year. The whole family came to our house.

5. That year was very cold. It snowed all Thanksgiving day.

6. I remember another thing about that Thanksgiving. My brother and I baked eight pies.

2 Adverbial clauses of time (page 54)

> ▶ An adverbial clause of time can come before or after the main clause. When it comes before the main clause, use a comma. When it comes after the main clause, don't use a comma: When Ginny and Tom met, they both lived in San Juan. BUT: Ginny and Tom met when they both lived in San Juan.
> ▶ The words *couple* and *family* are collective nouns. They are usually used with singular verbs: When a couple **gets** married, they often receive gifts. (NOT: When a couple ~~get~~ married, they often receive gifts.)

Combine the two sentences using the adverb in parentheses. Write one sentence with the adverbial clause before the main clause and another with the adverbial clause after the main clause.

1. Students complete their courses. A school holds a graduation ceremony. (after)
   a. After students complete their courses, a school holds a graduation ceremony.
   b. A school holds a graduation ceremony after students complete their courses.
2. Students gather to put on robes and special hats. The ceremony starts. (before)
   a.
   b.
3. Music plays. The students walk in a line to their seats. (when)
   a.
   b.
4. School officials and teachers make speeches. Students get their diplomas. (after)
   a.
   b.
5. The ceremony is finished. Students throw their hats into the air and cheer. (when)
   a.
   b.

Unit 9

1 Time contrasts (page 59)

> ▶ Use the modal *might* to say something is possible in the present or future: In a few years, movie theaters **might** not exist. = In a few years, maybe movie theaters won't exist.

Complete the conversation with the correct form of the verbs in parentheses. Use the past, present, or future tense.

A: I saw a fascinating program last night. It talked about the past, the present, and the future.

B: What kinds of things did it describe?

A: Well, for example, the normal work week in the 20th century .... (be) 35 hours. Nowadays, many people .... (work) more than 40 hours a week.

B: Well, that doesn't sound like progress.

A: You're right. But on the show, they said that most people .... (work) fewer hours in the future. They also talked about the way we shop. These days, many of us .... (shop) online. In the old days, there .... (be) no supermarkets, so people .... (have to) go to lots of different stores. In the future, people .... (do) all their shopping online.

B: I don't believe that.

A: Me neither. What about cars? Do you think people .... (still drive) cars a hundred years from now?

B: What did they say on the show?

A: They said that before the car, people .... (walk) everywhere. Nowadays, we .... (drive) everywhere. And that .... (not change).

2 Conditional sentences with *if* clauses (page 61)

> ▶ The *if* clause can come before or after the main clause: **If** I change my eating habits, I'll feel healthier. / I'll feel healthier **if** I change my eating habits. Always use a comma when the *if* clause comes before the main clause.
> ▶ For the future of *can*, use *will be able to*: If you save some money, you**'ll be able to buy** a car. (NOT: . . . you'll can buy a car.)
> ▶ For the future of *must*, use *will have to*: If you get a dog, you**'ll have to take care** of it. (NOT: . . . you'll must take care of it.)

Complete the sentences with the correct form of the verbs in parentheses.

1. If you .... *exercise* .... (exercise) more often, you ..*'ll feel*.................. (feel) more energetic.

2. If you .... (join) a gym, exercise .... (become) part of your routine.

3. You .... (not have to) worry about staying in shape if you .... (work out) three or four times a week.

4. If you .... (ride) a bike or .... (run) a few times a week, you .... (lose) weight and .... (gain) muscle.

5. You .... (sleep) better at night if you .... (exercise) regularly.

6. If you .... (start) exercising, you .... (might/not have) as many colds and other health problems.

Unit 10

1 Gerunds; short responses (page 65)

▶ Short responses with *so* and *neither* are ways of agreeing. The subject (noun or pronoun) comes after the verb: I love traveling. So **do I**. (NOT: So I do.) I can't stand talking on the phone. Neither **can I**. (NOT: Neither I can.)

Rewrite A's line using the words given. Then write an agreement for B.

1. I hate waiting in line at the bank. (can't stand)
   A: I can't stand waiting in line at the bank.
   B: Neither can I.
2. I don't like reading about politics or politicians. (interested in)
   A: ....
   B: ....
3. I can remember people's names. (good at)
   A: ....
   B: ....
4. I have no problem with working on weekends. (don't mind)
   A: ....
   B: ....
5. I love going for long walks in my free time. (enjoy)
   A: ....
   B: ....
6. I can't manage time well. (not good at)
   A: ....
   B: ....

2 Clauses with *because* (page 68)

▶ Clauses with *because* answer the question "Why?" or "Why not?": Why would you make a good flight attendant? I'd make a good flight attendant **because** I love traveling and I'm good with people.

Complete the sentences with *because* and the phrases in the box.

> I don't write very well
> I love arguing with people
> I'm afraid of flying
> ✓ I'm much too short
> I'm not patient enough to work with kids
> I'm really bad with numbers

1. I could never be a fashion model because I'm much too short.
2. I wouldn't make a good high school teacher ....
3. I wouldn't want to be a flight attendant ....
4. I could never be an accountant ....
5. I would make a bad journalist ....
6. I'd be an excellent lawyer ....

Unit 11

1 Passive with *by* (simple past) (page 73)

> ▶ The past participle of regular verbs is the same form as the simple past: Leonardo da Vinci **painted** *Mona Lisa* in 1503. *Mona Lisa* was **painted** by Leonardo da Vinci in 1503.
>
> ▶ The past participle of some – but not all – irregular verbs is the same form as the simple past: The Egyptians **built** the Pyramids. The Pyramids were **built** by the Egyptians. BUT Jane Austen **wrote** *Pride and Prejudice*. *Pride and Prejudice* was **written** by Jane Austen.

Change the sentences from active to passive with *by*.

1. The Chinese invented paper around 100 C.E.
   Paper was invented by the Chinese around 100 C.E.

2. Marie Curie discovered radium in 1898.
   ....

3. Dr. Felix Hoffmann made the first aspirin in 1899.
   ....

4. Tim Berners-Lee developed the World Wide Web in 1989.
   ....

5. William Herschel identified the planet Uranus in 1781.
   ....

6. Georges Bizet wrote the opera *Carmen* in the 1870s.
   ....

2 Passive without *by* (simple present) (page 75)

> ▶ When it is obvious or not important who is doing the action, don't use a *by* phrase: Both the Olympics and the World Cup are held every four years. (NOT: . . . are held ~~by people~~ . . .)

Complete the information with *is* or *are* and the past participle of the verbs in the box.

base
export
import
know
✓ speak
use

1. Portuguese – not Spanish – ......*is spoken*...... in Brazil.
2. Diamonds and gold from South Africa .... by countries all over the world.
3. The U.S. dollar .... in Puerto Rico.
4. Hawaii .... for its beautiful beaches.
5. Many electronic products .... by Japan and Korea. It's an important industry for these two countries.
6. The economy in many island countries, such as Jamaica, ... on tourism.

Unit 12

1 Past continuous vs. simple past (page 79)

> ▶ When the past continuous is used with the simple past, both actions happened at the same time but the past continuous action started earlier. The simple past action interrupted the past continuous action.

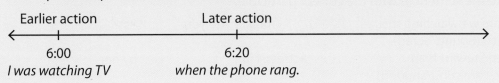

Earlier action   Later action

← ────────┼──────────────────────┼──────────── →

6:00   6:20
I was watching TV   *when the phone rang.*

Complete the conversations with the correct form of the verbs in parentheses. Use the past continuous or the simple past.

1. A: What happened to you?
   B: I ....*fell*......... (fall) while I ....*was jogging*.... (jog) in the park.
2. A: .... you .... (see) the storm yesterday?
   B: Yes. It .... (start) while I .... (drive) to work.
3. A: We finally .... (move) to a larger apartment.
   B: That's good. I know you .... (live) in a tiny place when your daughter .... (be) born.
4. A: My sister .... (have) a bad accident. She ....
      (hurt) her back when she .... (lift) weights at the gym.
   B: That .... (happen) to me last year, but I
      .... (not lift) weights. I .... (take)
      a boxing class and I .... (trip).

2 Present perfect continuous (page 81)

> ▶ The same time expressions used with the present perfect can also be used with the present perfect continuous. Don't confuse *for* and *since*: I've been working here **for** five years./I've been working here **since** 2010.

Complete the sentences with the present perfect continuous form of the verbs in parentheses.

1. A: What ....*have*........... you ....*been doing*.... all day?
   B: I .... (clean) the house, and Peter
      .... (watch) TV. He .... (not feel)
      very well lately.
   A: How .... you .... (feel) these days?
   B: I .... (feel) great. I .... (not eat)
      any junk food, and I .... (exercise) a lot. I
      .... (take) really good care of myself.
2. A: How long .... you and Joe .... (date)?
   B: We .... (go out) together for almost a year. Can
      you believe it?
   A: Maya and I .... (date) for even longer. I think it's
      time to get married. We .... (talk) about it a lot lately.
   B: Joe and I .... (not talk) about marriage, but I
      .... (think) about it.

Unit 13

1 Participles as adjectives (page 87)

▶ Adjectives ending in *–ing* are present participles. They are things that *cause* a feeling. Adjectives ending in *–ed* are past participles. They *express* the feeling.

Complete the sentences with the correct participle.

1. Why are we watching this ....*boring*........ movie? Are you ....*bored*.......... with it? (boring/bored)
2. Kristen Stewart is an .... actress. I'm .... by her talent. (amazing/amazed)
3. Are you .... in computer-generated special effects? The latest 3-D movies are very .... (interesting/interested)
4. I had an .... experience the last time I went to the movies. I started to cough, and I couldn't stop. I was really .... (embarrassing/embarrassed)
5. Julie and I saw the new *Pirates of the Caribbean* movie. I found it .... , but Julie didn't seem very .... by it. (amusing/amused)
6. Oh, I'm really .... with Jeremy right now. He took me to the most .... movie last night. I wanted to walk out after half an hour, but he wouldn't leave! (disgusting/disgusted)
7. Do you think sci-fi movie directors make their films .... intentionally? I get so .... by the complicated storylines and weird characters. (confusing/confused)
8. I think that great books make great movies. If I find a book .... , I'm usually .... by the movie also. (fascinating/fascinated)

2 Relative pronouns for people and things (page 89)

▶ Relative clauses give information about nouns. Don't use a personal pronoun in a relative clause: He's an actor **that** won two Oscars. (NOT: He's an actor that ~~he~~ won two Oscars.)

Complete the conversations. Use *that* for things and *who* for people.

A: How did you like the movie last night? Was it any good?

B: It wasn't bad, but it's not the kind of movie ......*that*...... makes you think. I like films .... have a strong message and interesting storylines.

A: How about the acting? Did you like the actors .... star in it?

B: Cameron Diaz is pretty good, actually.

A: Oh, she's the blonde actress .... was going out with Justin Timberlake.

B: Justin who? Who's that?

A: Oh, you know him. He's the one .... was in the band 'N Sync years ago. It was a "boy band" .... was popular in the 1990s.

B: I remember 'N Sync, but I don't remember the names of the guys .... were in the band.

A: Well, I loved Justin Timberlake when I was a kid. And he's not a bad actor. Did you see the movie *The Social Network*?

B: I did see that. It's about the guys .... started Facebook, right? I didn't realize Justin Timberlake was in it. Now I'll have to see it again!

Unit 14

1 Modals and adverbs (page 93)

▶ Use the modals *might/may*, *could*, and *must* and the adverbs *maybe/perhaps*, *possibly/probably*, and *definitely* when you aren't sure about what you're saying:
slight possibility: *might, may, maybe, perhaps*
possibility: *could, possibly, probably*
strong possibility: *must, definitely*

Rewrite each sentence in different ways, using the words in parentheses.

1. Perhaps it means she doesn't agree with you.
   a. (maybe) *Maybe it means she doesn't agree with you.* ....
   b. (might) ....
   c. (may) ....
2. That gesture could mean "Come here."
   a. (possibly) ....
   b. (probably) ....
3. That almost definitely means he doesn't understand you.
   a. (must) ....

2 Permission, obligation, and prohibition (page 95)

▶ Use *have/has* with *got to*: You**'ve got to** keep the door closed. (NOT: You ~~got to~~ keep the door closed.)

Complete the conversations with the words and phrases in the box. Use each word or phrase only once.

```
   are allowed to
   aren't allowed to
   can
 ✓ can't
   have to
   have got to
```

1. A: Oh, no! That sign says "No fishing." That means we ....*can't*......... fish here.
   B: You're right. We .... go somewhere else to fish. I think you .... fish in the pond on Cedar Road. Let's go there.
2. A: What does that sign mean?
   B: It means bad news for us. It means you .... bring dogs to the beach. We'd better take Buddy home.
3. A: Please don't leave your garbage here. You .... put it in the trash room down the hall. That's one of the building's rules.
   B: I'm really sorry.
4. A: You .... put your bike in the bike room downstairs, if you want. It's much safer than locking it up outside.
   B: Oh, that's great! I'll do that. I didn't know about the bike room.

Unit 15

1 Unreal conditional sentences with *if* clauses (page 101)

> ▶ The clauses in unreal conditional sentences can come in either order. Don't use a comma when the *if* clause comes second: **If** I won the lottery, I'd share the money with my family./I'd share the money with my family **if** I won the lottery.

Complete the conversation with the correct form of the verbs in parentheses.

1. A: If a friend ....asked........ (ask) to borrow some money, what ....would.... you ......say...... (say)?

   B: Well, if I .... (have) any extra money that month, I .... probably .... (give) it to her.

2. A: What .... you .... (do) if someone .... (give) you a million dollars?

   B: Hmm, I'm not sure. I .... (buy) a lot of nice clothes and jewelry, or I .... (spend) some and .... (give) some away, or I .... (put) it all in the bank.

3. A: If you .... (think) a friend was doing something dangerous, ... you .... (say) something to him, or .... you .... (keep) quiet?

   B: I .... definitely .... (talk) to my friend about it.

4. A: What .... you .... (do) if you .... (have) a problem with your boss?

   B: That's a hard one. If that .... (happen), I .... (talk) to the Human Resources department about it, or I .... just .... (sit down) with my boss and .... (talk) about the situation.

2 Past modals (page 103)

> ▶ Use *should have* and *would have* for all subjects. They don't change form: He **should have called** sooner. (NOT: He should has called sooner.)

Read the situations. Use the words in parentheses to write opinions and suggestions.

1. My neighbor had a party last night. It was very loud, so I called the police.
   (you / speak / to your neighbor first)
   You should have spoken to your neighbor first.

2. The mail carrier put someone else's mail in my box. I threw it away.
   (you / write / a note and leave / the mail in your box)
   ....

3. My sister asked if I liked her new dress. It didn't look good on her, but I said it did. (I / tell her the truth)
   ....

4. A salesperson called me last night. I didn't want to buy anything, but I let her talk to me for almost half an hour.
   (I / tell her I'm not interested / hang up)
   ....

Unit 16

1 Reported speech: requests (page 107)

▶ When a reported request is negative, *not* comes before *to*: Don't leave your wet towel on the floor. She told me **not to leave** my wet towel on the floor. (NOT: She told me ~~to not~~ leave my wet towel on the floor.)

Harry's roommate, Tyler, is making some requests. Read what Tyler said to Harry. Write the requests with the verb in parentheses and reported speech.

1. "Can you put away your clean clothes?" (ask)
   Tyler asked Harry to put away his clean clothes.

2. "Meet me in the cafeteria at school at noon." (say)
   ....

3. "Don't leave your shoes in the living room." (tell)
   ....

4. "Hang up your wet towels." (say)
   ....

5. "Could you stop using my phone?" (ask)
   ....

6. "Make your bed on weekdays." (tell)
   ....

7. "Don't eat my food." (say)
   ....

8. "Be a better roommate!" (tell)
   ....

2 Reported speech: statements (page 109)

▶ The tense of the introducing verb (*ask, say, tell*) changes when the sentence is reported: simple present → simple past; present continuous → past continuous; present perfect → past perfect. Modals change, too: *can* → *could*; *will* → *would*; *may* → *might*.

Bill and Kathy are having a barbecue on Sunday. They're upset because a lot of their friends can't come. Read what their friends said. Change the excuses into reported speech.

1. Lori: "I have to visit my grandparents that day."
   Lori said that she had to visit her grandparents that day.

2. Mario: "I'm going to a play on Sunday."
   ....

3. Julia: "I've promised to take my brother to the movies that day."
   ....

4. Daniel: "I can't come. I have to study for a huge exam on Monday."
   ....

5. The neighbors: "We'll be out of town all weekend."
   ....

6. Alice: "I may have to babysit my nephew."
   ....

Grammar plus answer key

Unit 1

1 Past tense

2. did you grow up/are you from
3. Did you live
4. When did you move
5. did you go
6. when did you come/get

2 Used to

1. A: Hey, Dad. What kinds of clothes **did you use to** wear – you know, when you were a kid?
   B: Oh, we **used to** wear jeans and T-shirts – like you kids do now.
   A: Really? **Did** Mom **use to** dress like that, too?
   B: No, not really. She never **used to** like wearing pants. She always **used to** wear skirts and dresses.
2. A: **Did** you **use to** play a sport when you were a kid?
   B: Well, I **used to** be a swimmer. My sister and I **used to** swim on a team.
   A: Wow, that's cool! Were you good?
   B: Yeah. I **used to** win gold medals all the time. And my sister **used to** be the fastest swimmer on the team.

Unit 2

1 Expressions of quantity

1. A: There's **too much** traffic in this city. There should be **fewer** cars downtown.
   B: The problem is there **isn't** enough public transportation.
   A: You're right. We should have more **buses**. There **aren't** enough of them during rush hour.
2. A: How do you like your new neighborhood?
   B: It's terrible, actually. There's **too much** noise and **too little** parking.
   A: That's too bad. There **aren't** enough parking spaces in my neighborhood either.
3. A: Did you hear about the changes to the city center? Starting next month, there will be more bicycle **lanes** and **less** street parking.
   B: That's good. There **is too much** pollution downtown. I'm sure there will be **fewer** accidents, too.
   A: That's true.

2 Indirect questions from Wh-questions

Answers may vary. Some possible answers:

2. And could you **tell me where I can find a good restaurant**?
3. Do you **know what the name of the restaurant is**?
4. Can you **tell me what type of food they serve**?
5. Do you **know what time the restaurant opens**?

Unit 3

1 Evaluations and comparisons

A

Answers may vary. Some possible answers:

2. This street isn't quiet enough.
   This street is too noisy.
3. This house doesn't have enough bedrooms.
   This house is too small for us.
   This house has too few bedrooms for us.
4. This living room isn't spacious enough.
   This living room doesn't have enough space.
   This living room is too cramped/small.

B

Answers may vary. Some possible answers:

2. My old neighborhood isn't as safe as this one.
3. This apartment has (just) as much privacy as my old one.
4. My rent isn't as high as it used to be.

2 Wish

2. f   3. b   4. e   5. a   6. d

Unit 4

1 Simple past vs. present perfect

1. A: What **did you have** for dinner last night?
   B: I **tried** Indian food for the first time. **Have you ever had** it?
   A: A friend and I **ate** at an Indian restaurant just last week. It **was** delicious!
2. A: **Have you ever taken** a cooking class?
   B: No, **I haven't**. How about you?
   A: I **have taken** a few classes. My last class **was** in December. We **learned** how to make some wonderful Spanish dishes.
3. A: I **watched** a great cooking show on TV yesterday.
   B: Really? I **have never seen** a cooking show. **Was it** boring?
   A: No, it **wasn't**. It **was** very interesting!

2 Sequence adverbs

Step 1: First, put 2 pounds of chopped beef in a bowl.
Step 2: Then add salt and pepper to the meat in the bowl.
Step 3: Next, mix the meat and the salt and pepper together.
Step 4: After that, form the meat into four burgers with your hands.
Step 5: Finally, put the burgers in a pan and cook for ten minutes.

Unit 5

1 Future with *be going to* and *will*

B: I'm not sure. I'm really tired, so I probably **won't do** anything exciting. Maybe I'**ll see** a movie on Saturday. How about you? How **are you going to spend** your weekend?

A: My wife and I **are going to do** some work on our house. We'**re going to paint** the living room on Saturday. On Sunday, we'**re going to clean** all the rugs.

B: **Are(n't) you going to do** anything fun?

A: Oh, I think we'**ll have/'re going to have** a lot of fun. We like working around the house. And Sunday's my birthday, so we'**re going to have** dinner at my favorite Italian restaurant.

B: Now that sounds like fun!

2 Modals for necessity and suggestions

1. You **must** show identification at the airport. They won't allow you on a plane without an official ID.
2. Your ID **needs to** have a picture of you on it. It's required.
3. The picture of you **has to** be recent. They won't accept an old photo.
4. Travelers **should** get to the airport at least two hours before their flight. It's not a good idea to get there later than that.
5. All travelers **have to** go through airport security. It's necessary for passenger safety.
6. Many airlines don't serve food, so passengers on long flights probably **ought to** buy something to eat at the airport.

Unit 6

1 Two-part verbs; *will* for responding to requests

2. A: Turn on the lights, please.
   B: OK. I'll turn them on.
3. A: Please turn down your music.
   B: OK. I'll turn it down.
4. A: Clean the kitchen up, please.
   B: OK. I'll clean it up.
5. A: Turn your phone off, please.
   B: OK. I'll turn it off.

2 Requests with modals and *Would you mind . . . ?*

2. Would you mind putting your shoes by the door?
3. Would you mind not leaving dishes in the sink?
4. Can you change the TV channel?
5. Would you mind not playing ball inside?
6. Would you mind cleaning up your mess?
7. Can you put away the clean towels?
8. Could you pick up your things?

Unit 7

1 Infinitives and gerunds for uses and purposes

2. a. I use my smartphone/it to take pictures.
   b. I use my smartphone/it for taking pictures.
3. a. You use a flash drive/it to back up files.
   b. You use a flash drive/it for backing up files.
4. a. He would only use a laptop/it to watch movies and play games.
   b. He would only use a laptop/it for watching movies and playing games.
5. a. I use my computer/it to shop online and do research.
   b. I use my computer/it for shopping online and doing research.

2 Imperatives and infinitives for giving suggestions

2. Try not to talk on the phone when you're in an elevator.
3. Be sure not to eat or drink anything when you're at the computer.
4. Remember to clean your computer screen and keyboard once a week.
5. Make sure not to use your tablet outside when it's raining.
6. When the bell rings to start class, be sure to put your music player away!

Unit 8

1 Relative clauses of time

2. It's a wonderful time when people give thanks for the good things in their lives.
3. It's a day when everyone eats much more than usual.
4. I remember one particular year when the whole family came to our house.
5. That was a very cold year/Thanksgiving when it snowed all (Thanksgiving) day.
6. That was also the year/Thanksgiving when my brother and I baked eight pies.

2 Adverbial clauses of time

2. a. Students gather to put on robes and special hats before the ceremony starts.
   b. Before the ceremony starts, students gather to put on robes and special hats.
3. a. When the music plays, the students walk in a line to their seats.
   b. The students walk in a line to their seats when the music plays.
4. a. After school officials and teachers make speeches, students get their diplomas.
   b. Students get their diplomas after school officials and teachers make speeches.
5. a. When the ceremony is finished, students throw their hats into the air and cheer.
   b. Students throw their hats into the air and cheer when the ceremony is finished.

Unit 9

1 Time contrasts

A: I saw a fascinating program last night. It talked about the past, the present, and the future.

B: What kinds of things did it describe?

A: Well, for example, the normal work week in the 20th century **was** 35 hours. Nowadays, many people **work/are working** more than 40 hours a week.

B: Well, that doesn't sound like progress.

A: You're right. On the show, they said that most people **will work/might work** fewer hours in the future. They also talked about the way we shop. These days, many of us **shop** online. In the old days, there **were** no supermarkets, so people **had to/used to have to go** to lots of different stores. In the future, people **will do/are going to do** all their shopping online.

B: I don't believe that.

A: Me neither. What about cars? Do you think people **will still drive/are still going to drive** cars a hundred years from now?

B: What did they say on the show?

A: They said that before the car, people **used to walk/walked** everywhere. Nowadays, we drive everywhere. And that **isn't going to change/'s not going to change/won't change.**

2 Conditional sentences with *if* clauses

2. If you join a gym, exercise will become part of your routine.
3. You won't have to worry about staying in shape if you work out three or four times a week.
4. If you ride a bike or run a few times a week, you'll lose weight and gain muscle.
5. You'll sleep better at night if you exercise regularly.
6. If you start exercising, you might not have as many colds and other health problems.

Unit 10

1 Gerunds; short responses

2. A: I'm not interested in reading about politics or politicians.
   B: Neither am I.
3. A: I'm good at remembering people's names.
   B: So am I.
4. A: I don't mind working on weekends.
   B: Neither do I.
5. A: I enjoy going for long walks in my free time.
   B: So do I.
6. A: I'm not good at managing time well.
   B: Neither am I.

2 Clauses with *because*

2. I wouldn't make a good high school teacher **because I'm not patient enough to work with kids.**
3. I wouldn't want to be a flight attendant **because I'm afraid of flying.**
4. I could never be an accountant **because I'm really bad with numbers.**
5. I would make a bad journalist **because I don't write very well.**
6. I'd be an excellent lawyer **because I love arguing with people.**

Unit 11

1 Passive with *by* (simple past)

2. Radium was discovered by Marie Curie in 1898.
3. The first aspirin was made by Dr. Felix Hoffmann in 1899.
4. The World Wide Web was developed by Tim Berners-Lee in 1989.
5. The planet Uranus was identified in 1781 by William Herschel.
6. The opera *Carmen* was written by Georges Bizet in the 1870s.

2 Passive without *by* (simple present)

2. Diamonds and gold from South Africa **are imported** by countries all over the world.
3. The U.S. dollar **is used** in Puerto Rico.
4. Hawaii **is known** for its beautiful beaches.
5. Many electronic products **are exported** by Japan and Korea. It's an important industry for these two countries.
6. The economy in many island countries, such as Jamaica, **is based** on tourism.

Unit 12

1 Past continuous vs. simple past

2. A: **Did** you **see** the storm yesterday?
   B: Yes! It **started** while I **was driving** to work.
3. A: We finally **moved** to a larger apartment.
   B: That's good. I know you **were living** in a tiny place when your daughter **was** born.
4. A: My sister **had** a bad accident. She **hurt** her back when she **was lifting** weights at the gym.
   B: That **happened** to me last year, but I **wasn't lifting** weights. I **was taking** a boxing class and I **tripped.**

2 Present perfect continuous

1. A: What **have** you **been doing** all day?
   B: I**'ve been cleaning** the house, and Peter **has been watching** TV. He **hasn't been feeling** very well lately.
   A: How **have** you **been feeling** these days?
   B: I**'ve been feeling** great. I **haven't been eating** any junk food, and I**'ve been exercising** a lot. I**'ve been taking** really good care of myself.
2. A: How long **have** you and Joe **been dating**?
   B: We**'ve been going out** together for almost a year. Can you believe it?
   A: Maya and I **have been dating** for even longer. I think it's time to get married. We**'ve been talking** about it a lot lately.
   B: Joe and I **haven't been talking** about marriage, but I**'ve been thinking** about it.

Unit 13

1 Participles as adjectives

2. Kristen Stewart is an **amazing** actress. I'm **amazed** by her talent.
3. Are you **interested** in computer-generated special effects? The latest 3D movies are very **interesting**.

4. I had an **embarrassing** experience the last time I went to the movies. I started to cough, and I couldn't stop. I was really **embarrassed**.
5. Julie and I saw the new *Pirates of the Caribbean* movie. I found it **amusing**, but Julie didn't seem very **amused** by it.
6. Oh, I'm really **disgusted** with Jeremy right now. He took me to the most **disgusting** movie last night. I wanted to walk out after half an hour, but he wouldn't leave!
7. Do you think sci-fi movie directors make their films **confusing** intentionally? I get so **confused** by the complicated storylines and weird characters.
8. I think that great books make great movies. If I find a book **fascinating**, I'm usually **fascinated** by the movie also.

2 Relative clauses for people and things

A: How did you like the movie last night? Was it any good?
B: It wasn't bad, but it's not the kind of movie **that** makes you think. I like films **that** have a strong message and interesting storylines.
A: How about the acting? Did you like the actors **who** star in it?
B: Cameron Diaz is pretty good, actually.
A: Oh, she's the blonde actress **who** was going out with Justin Timberlake.
B: Justin who? Who's that?
A: Oh, you know him. He's the one **who** was in the band 'N Sync years ago. It was a "boy band" **that** was popular in the 1990s.
B: I remember 'N Sync, but I don't remember the names of the guys **who** were in the band.
A: Well, I loved Justin Timberlake when I was a kid. And he's not a bad actor. Did you see the movie *The Social Network*?
B: I did see that. It's about the guys **who** started Facebook, right? I didn't realize Justin Timberlake was in it. Now I'll have to see it again!

Unit 14

1 Modals and adverbs

1. a. Maybe it means she doesn't agree with you.
   b. It might mean she doesn't agree with you.
   c. It may mean she doesn't agree with you.
2. a. That gesture possibly means "Come here."
   b. That gesture probably means "Come here."
3. a. That must mean he doesn't understand you.

2 Permission, obligation, and prohibition

1. A: Oh, no! That sign says "No fishing." That means we **can't** fish here.
   B: You're right. We**'ve got to/have to** go somewhere else to fish. I think **you're allowed to/can** fish in the pond on Cedar Road. Let's go there.
2. A: What does that sign mean?
   B: It means bad news for us. It means you **aren't allowed to** bring dogs to the beach. We'd better take Buddy home.
3. A: Please don't leave your garbage here. You**'ve got to/have to** put it in the trash room down the hall. That's one of the building's rules.
   B: I'm really sorry.

4. A: You **can** put your bike in the bike room downstairs, if you want. It's much safer than locking it up outside.
   B: Oh, that's great! I'll do that. I didn't know about the bike room.

Unit 15

1 Unreal conditional sentences with *if*

1. A: If a friend **asked** to borrow some money, what **would** you **say**?
   B: Well, if I **had** any extra money that month, I **would** probably **give** it to her.
2. A: What **would/could** you **do** if someone **gave** you a million dollars?
   B: Hmm, I'm not sure. I **could/might buy** a lot of nice clothes and jewelry, or I **could/might spend** some and **give** some away, or I **could/might put** it all in the bank.
3. A: If you **thought** a friend was doing something dangerous, **would** you **say** something to him, or **would** you **keep** quiet?
   B: I **would** definitely **talk** to my friend about it.
4. A: What **would** you **do** if you **had** a problem with your boss?
   B: That's a hard one. If that **happened**, I **might talk** to the Human Resources department about it, or I **might/could** just **sit down** with my boss and **talk** about the situation.

2 Past modals

2. You should have written a note and left the mail in your box.
3. I would have told her the truth.
4. I would have told her I wasn't interested and hung up (the phone).

Unit 16

1 Reported speech: requests

2. Tyler said to meet him in the cafeteria at school at noon.
3. Tyler told him/Harry not to leave his shoes in the living room.
4. Tyler said to hang up his wet towels.
5. Tyler asked him/Harry to stop using his/Tyler's phone.
6. Tyler told him/Harry to make his bed on weekdays.
7. Tyler said not to eat his/Tyler's food.
8. Tyler told him/Harry to be a better roommate.

2 Reported speech: statements

1. Lori said (that) she had to visit her grandparents that day.
   Lori told them (that) she had to visit her grandparents that day.
2. Mario said/told them (that) he was going to a play on Sunday.
3. Julia said/told them (that) she had promised to take her brother to the movies that day.
4. Daniel said/told them (that) he couldn't come because he had to study for a huge exam on Monday.
5. The neighbors said/told them (that) they would be out of town all weekend.
6. Alice said/told them (that) she might have to babysit her nephew.

Credits

Illustrations

Andrezzinho: 16 (*top*), 43 (*top*), 62; **Ilias Arahovitis:** 37; **Mark Collins:** v, 16 (*bottom*), 36 (*top*), 41, 67 (*top*); **Carlos Diaz:** 39, 46, 93 (*bottom*), 104 (*center*), 114; **Jada Fitch:** 65, 119; **Travis Foster:** 20, 40 (*top*), 90 (*top*), 97 (*center*), 116 (*bottom*); **Chuck Gonzales:** 2, 30 (*top*), 64 (*bottom*), 106, 117; **Jim Haynes:** 36 (*bottom*), 75, 79, 99; **Trevor Keen:** 38, 61, 102, 121; **Jim Kelly:** 95 (*bottom earbuds, cell phone*) ; **Joanna Kerr:** 123; **KJA-artists:** 124 (*bottom*), 130; **Shelton Leong:** 22 (*bottom*), 58 (*bottom*), 108, 109; **Karen Minot:** 25 (*top*), 27, 32, 64 (*top*), 68, 72 (*top*), 76, 78, 90 (*bottom*), 105, 118, 129, 131; **Rob Schuster:** 8, 13, 18, 35, 40 (*bottom*), 44 (*early smartphone*), 50, 58 (*top*), 67 (*bottom*), 77, 86, 97, 122, 125; **Daniel Vasconcellos:** 15, 82, 110, 112; **Brad Walker:** 81, 100 (*bottom*); **Sam Whitehead:** 5, 6, 33, 43 (*bottom*), 53, 54, 92 (*bottom*), 93 (*top*), 127; **Jeff Wong:** 60; **James Yamasaki:** 19, 25 (*bottom*), 80, 94, 111; 128; **Rose Zgodzinski:** 2, 10, 22 (*top*), 30 (*top*), 44 (*top*), 55, 69, 78 (*top*), 92 (*top*), 120, 124 (*top*); **Carol Zuber-Mallison:** 7, 21, 26, 44 (*bottom*), 49, 63, 83, 85, 91, 100 (*top*), 104 (*bottom*), 116 (*top*), 126

Photos

2 (*left*) © Leslie Banks/iStockphoto; (*right*) © Jacqueline Veissid/Lifesize/Getty Images
3 © MIXA/Getty Images
6 © Stretch Photography/Blend Images/age fotostock
7 (*clockwise from top*) © Steve Granitz/WireImage/Getty Images; © MGM Studios/Moviepix/Getty Images; © Photos 12/Alamy
8 (*top middle*) © Ilene MacDonald/Alamy; (*top right*) © Temmuz Can Arsiray/iStockphoto; (*bottom, clockwise from left*) © Jeff Morgan 09/Alamy; © Peter Treanor/Alamy; © Daniel Borzynski/Alamy
9 B. O'Kane/Alamy
11 © Zero Creatives/Cultura/Getty Images
13 (*top row*) © AP Photo/Uwe Lein; © AP Photo/Kydpl Kyodo; © Andrew Robinson/Alamy; © Courtesy of Wheelman Inc.
14 © Superstock/Getty Images
17 (*left to right*) © Imagemore Co. Ltd./Getty Images; © Niels Poulsen Mus/Alamy
18 © Yusuke Nakanishi/Aflo Foto Agency/Alamy
19 © Creatas/Punchstock
21 © Image100/age fotostock
22 (*top row*) © Topic Photo Agency/age fotostock; © Nico Tondini/age fotostock; © Eising/Bon Appetit/Alamy; © JTB Photo/SuperStock
23 © Juice Images/Alamy
24 (*top right*) © Jupiter Images/Foodpix/Getty Images; (*middle row*) © iStockphoto/Thinkstock; © Dave King/Dorling Kindersley/Getty Images; © Olga Utlyakova/iStockphoto; © funkyfood London-Paul Williams/Alamy; © John Kelly/Food Image Source/StockFood; © Eiichi Onodera/Getty Images
25 (*top left*) © Archive Photos/Stringer/Getty Images; (*middle row*) © George Kerrigan
26 (*top row*) © Shipes/Shooter/StockFood; © Olivier Blondeau/iStockphoto; © Brent Melton/iStockphoto; © Boris Ryzhkov/iStockphoto; © Morten Olsen/iStockphoto; (*middle right*) © Asiaselects/Getty Images; (*bottom right*) © Debbi Smirnoff/iStockphoto
27 (*top right*) © Altrendo/Getty Images; (*middle right*) © Sean Justice/Getty Images
29 (*middle right*) © Jiri Hera/Shutterstock; (*bottom right*) © AP Photo/Shizuo Kambayashi
30 (*top row*) © Travelscape Images/Alamy; © Chicasso/Blend/Getty Images; © i love images/Veer; © Larry Williams/LWA/Blend Images/Alamy
31 © Julien Capmeil/Photonica/Getty Images
34 (*middle right*) © Irene Alastruey/age fotostock; (*bottom left*) © Teresa Kasprzycka/Shutterstock
35 © Jeff Greenberg/Alamy
38 © UpperCut Images/Getty Images
42 © Tyler Stableford/Stone/Getty Images
44 (*clockwise from left*) © Jowita Stachowiak/iStockphoto; © SSPL/Getty Images; © RubberBall/Alamy; © David J. Green-studio/Alamy; © iStockphoto/Thinkstock; © Suto Norbert Zsolt/Shutterstock; © 7505811966/Shutterstock; © Oleksiy Mark/Shutterstock
45 (*top right*) © Mark Evans/iStockphoto; (*middle right*) © Schiller/F1online digitale Bildagentur GmbH/Alamy
46 © Sullivan/Corbis
47 (*top right*) © Jupiterimages/Comstock Images/Getty Images; (*bottom right, top to bottom*) © Miles Boyer/Shutterstock; © Mark Evans/iStockphoto; © broker/Veer
48 (*top row*) © mbbirdy/iStockphoto; © Maxim Pavlov/Veer; © Scanrail/Fotolia; © gabyjalbert/iStockphoto; © Christophe Testi/Shutterstock; (*bottom right*) © Monashee Frantz/Ojo Images/age fotostock
49 (*right, top to bottom*) © Jurgen Wiesler/Imagebroker/Alamy; © Alfaguarilla/Shutterstock

50 (*top row*) © Roberto Gerometta/Lonely Planet Images/Getty Images; © David Hancock/Alamy; © Toru Yamanaka/AFP/Getty Images; © Tipograffias/Shutterstock
51 (*clockwise from top*) © Michael Flippo/Fotolia; © Olga Lyubkina/iStockphoto; © DNY59/iStockphoto
52 (*top left*) © Masterfile; (*middle*) © AP Photo/Ibrahim Usta; (*middle right*) © Jack Hollingsworth/Asia Images//age fotostock; (*bottom right*) © Andy Chen/Flickr/Getty Images
53 © Christian Kober/AWL Images /Getty Images
55 (*top left*) © AP Photo/Collin Reid; (*top right*) © Michel Setboun/Corbis; (*middle left*) © Mickael David/Author's Image Ltd/Alamy; (*middle right*) © Ville Myllynen/AFP/Getty Images/NEWSCOM
56 © iStockphoto/Thinkstock
57 © Esbin Anderson/Photo Network/Alamy
58 (*top row*) © FPG/Retrofile/Getty Images; © Ariel Skelley/Blend Images/Corbis; © Colin Anderson/Blend Images/Corbis
59 © Evening Standard/Stringer/Hulton Archive /Getty Images
60 © Engine Images/Fotolia
63 © Lane Oatey/Getty Images
67 (*bottom row*) © PBNJ Productions/Blend Images/Getty Images; © imagebroker.net/SuperStock; © Joe McBride/Stone/Getty Images
69 © Peter Dazeley/Photographer's Choice/Getty Images
71 (*middle row*) © Peter Dazeley/The Image Bank/Getty Images; © Topic Photo Agency/age fotostock; © Digital Vision/Photodisc/Thinkstock
72 (*top row*) © Dinodia/age fotostock; © Angelo Cavalli/age fotostock; © Jean-Paul Azam/The Image Bank/Getty Images; © Siegfried Layda/Photographer's Choice/Getty Images; © Renault Philippe/Hemis/Alamy; (*bottom right*) © Mathias Beinling/Alamy
73 © Javier Soriano/AFP/Getty Images
74 (*middle row*) © iStockphoto/Thinkstock; © Takashi Katahira/Amana Images/Corbis; © Keren Su/Corbis
76 (*right, top to bottom*) © Mardagada/Alamy; © Timothy Fadek/Corbis; (*bottom right*) © Jim Holmes/Axiom Photographic Agency/Getty Images
77 (*top row*) © Yvette Cardozo/Alamy; © Robert Harding Picture Library/SuperStock; © Oliver Berg/epa/Corbis
78 (*top row*) © Jeff Sarpa/StockFood Creative/Getty Images; © Stocksnapper/Alamy; © Pando Hall/Photographer's Choice/Getty Images; (*bottom left*) © Cultura Creative/Alamy
80 © AP Photo/Xie zhengyi/Imaginechina
83 (*top right*) © La Belle Kinoise/AFP/Getty Images/NEWSCOM; (*middle left*) © Urman Lionel/SIPA/NEWSCOM
84 © 20th Century Fox Film Corp./Everett Collection
86 (*left, top to bottom*) © AF archive/Alamy; © 20th Century Fox Film Corp./Everett Collection; (*right, top to bottom*) © AP Photo/Murray Close; © 20th Century Fox Film Corp./Everett Collection; (*bottom right*) © Mario Anzuoni/Reuters/Corbis
87 © Vera Anderson/WireImage/Getty Images
89 © Razorpix/Alamy
90 © David James/Twentieth Century Fox/Everett Collection
91 © Richard Foreman/Twentieth Century Fox Film Corp./Photofest
104 © Design Pics/Punchstock
107 © Photodisc/Getty Images
115 (*all*) (*Rio de Janeiro*) © John Banagan/age fotostock; (*Cairo*) © Robin Laurance/Look/age fotostock; (*Hong Kong*) © Martyn Vickery/Alamy; (*Salzburg*) © Lebrecht Music and Arts Photo Library/Alamy
118 © H.Mark Weidman Photography/Alamy
120 © Corbis flirt/Alamy
122 (*bottom row*) © Creatas Images/Thinkstock; © Chan Leong Hin/age fotostock; © Jay Newman/LWA/Blend Images/Getty Images
126 (*Heads, Tails*) © Jeffrey Kuan/iStockphoto